THE INTERNATIONAL JOURNAL FOR THE PSYCHOLOGY OF RELIGION, *12*(4), 213–215
Copyright © 2002, Lawrence Erlbaum Associates, Inc.

EDITORS' NOTE

This special issue of *The International Journal for the Psychology of Religion*, organized around the theme, "From Conflict to Dialogue: Examining Western and Islamic Approaches in Psychology of Religion," is an outgrowth of The First International Congress on Religion and Mental Health held in Tehran, Islamic Republic of Iran, from April 16–19, 2001. The issue evolved from what was initially intended to be a brief report on the conference. Helmut Reich was asked to assemble some of the authors of papers at the conference in order to have them coauthor a statement that would describe the Congress and assess the nature of the papers given. We decided that it would be helpful and appropriate to include authors who represent both a Western and an Islamic perspective.

Khalili, Murken, Reich, Shah, and Vahabzadeh were invited to participate in the author team. It was felt that this group could cogently and clearly engage the issues and that any clear differences of point of view would be expressed, because, although all authors have done their post-graduate studies in Western universities, two of them work in Western Europe (Murken in Germany; Reich in Switzerland) and three of them work in Islamic countries (Khalili and Vahabzadeh in Iran; Shah in Malaysia).

THE TECHNICAL USE OF SECULAR

What began as an effort to publish a short documentary note developed over the course of months of exchange with and between the authors into a set of two longer articles that engage the issues between models of Western psychology of religion and an Islamic religious psychology. The issues involved are expressions of fundamental differences in the conceptualizations of science and religion and the relation between a secular model of psychology of religion and a particular religious psychology.

Because there are some views within Islam that secular connotes materialism, modernity, and the secularization of society, that secular notions assume that religion is impractical and full of contradictions, and that such notions corrupt societies and Islamic society in particular, we think it is necessary to explain how we use this term and how it is understood in the articles in this journal issue. *Secular* is used as a purely technical term, and in the present context merely indicates that research (a) is based on the assumption that religion is situated at the same level as other sectors of activity such as health services, economics, politics, etc, each having its own distinctness and rationality, and (b) is carried out by formulating falsifiable hypotheses which are tested empirically. Therefore, *secular* as used in this journal issue does not concern historical analyses, does not involve criticism of religion, and does not imply the acceptance of, nor the rejection of, one overarching worldview. There are many psychologists of religion who have adopted a secular model of psychology of religion for their research, although they are religious believers and lead their lives accordingly. While being aware that the aforementioned version of Islamic understanding and interpretation of *secular* is comprehensible, historically speaking, and that there are differing views of such understanding or interpretation, we are also aware of justified critiques of religion. Our view is that dialogue should concentrate on the best of differing efforts, not on the worst.

As a journal concerned with the psychological understanding of how religion works in people's lives, the *Journal* is neutral with respect to the truth claims and the beliefs of specific religions. However, it sees a great need for open exchange of ideas among those with differing views.

Some of the views expressed reflect deep beliefs and values held by each author. We have taken special care to make sure that the writing expresses the author's own opinion. We have also protected each author's right to express his or her personal point of view in his or her own way. Although some of the statements may seem unusual to some readers, we nevertheless decided that it is best, in the interest of academic freedom, intellectual integrity, and open dialogue, to let each author's statements and point of view be expressed and stand or fall on their own.

The two articles that follow the editors' introduction are the outcome of many separate communications among the authors and between the authors and the editors. They are, therefore, presented that way, with each author signing his or her own sections of the article. This set the stage for a true dialogue, in which each one could address remarks by each of the others. Therefore, the points of view expressed are those of the author of each individual section of the articles, and do not represent the view of the editor of the journal, the journal itself, or the publisher.

IN THE AFTERMATH OF SEPTEMBER 11, 2001

The report on The First International Congress on Religion and Mental Health in Tehran was organized and planned before the terrible and regrettable events in New York, Pennsylvania, and Washington, D.C., on September 11, 2001. Through their public discussion, these events have hopefully led to an enlarged understanding and awareness of Islam and of what it does and does not teach. In this process, marked differences in the interpretation of the September 11, 2001 events, as well as important lacunae concerning the details of Islamic teachings, have become apparent, particularly in the West. These varying perspectives indicate the need for us to communicate with and mutually inform each other, to research the issues together and bring greater understanding to all of us.

If the psychology of religion wishes to research and understand all religions worldwide, then dialogue between researchers having different cultural perspectives is indispensable. The challenge for scholars in the psychology of religion is to neither present one's own view as an apologetic, nor to discard the perspectives of others as merely apologetic, but instead to respect them as the basis of their perception and conceptualization of the world. The authors in this issue attempt to do this. Accurate knowledge of the psychological processes in human religiousness is what we strive for. We are therefore unpretentious about our own points of view, and open about listening to the views of others.

Islam is one of the world's largest and most diverse religions, and like Christianity and Judaism, its followers hold many different views about its teachings. We hope that the following two articles will help to convey this within the context of a discussion about what the psychology of religion is and is not.

RESEARCH, GEOGRAPHICAL REPRESENTATION, AND REVIEW

We are fortunate to have three additional components to this special issue. The research team of Watson, Ghorbani, Davison, Bing, Hood, and Ghramaleki presents a thorough empirical report that is rich in data on religious orientation and various mental health measures in Iran and the United States. In a timely contribution, Dr. Haque and Ms. Masuan summarize an Islamic religious psychology and the status of the interrelationships between psychology and religion in Malaysia. Dr. Rubin provides an insightful review of a recently published book concerned with the religious bases of terrorism and the global rise of religious violence.

ACKNOWLEDGMENTS

Our appreciation goes to all authors. We thank especially the authors of the first two articles for their willingness to write on what were at times sensitive and controversial matters that confronted deeply held opinions and ideas. All were firmly challenged during the process. We also appreciate the publisher, Lawrence Erlbaum Associates, Inc., for their efforts to publish this journal on an early production schedule. Special thanks are due Dr. Kathleen O'Connor. Her insight and advice were invaluable during the final editing process.

K. Helmut Reich and Raymond F. Paloutzian

THE INTERNATIONAL JOURNAL FOR THE PSYCHOLOGY OF RELIGION, *12*(4), 217–237

INVITED ESSAY

Religion and Mental Health in Cultural Perspective: Observations and Reflections After The First International Congress on Religion and Mental Health, Tehran, 16–19 April 2001

Shiva Khalili

National Research Center of Medical Science, Tehran

Sebastian Murken

*Center for Psychological and Psychosomatic Research
University of Trier, Germany*

K. Helmut Reich

*Department of Education
University of Fribourg, Switzerland*

Ashiq Ali Shah

*Department of Psychology
International Islamic University Malaysia, Kuala Lumpur*

Abdolvahab Vahabzadeh

*Neuroscience Division
Iranian University of Medical Sciences, Tehran*

Requests for reprints should be sent to Dr. K. Helmut Reich, Department of Education, University of Fribourg, Rue de Faucigny 2, CH-1700 Fribourg, Switzerland. E-mail: helmut.reich@unifr.ch

This article first describes and then discusses The First International Congress on Religion and Mental Health held in Tehran, Islamic Republic of Iran, from 16-19 April 2001. With 242 papers and posters received and 158 selected for presentation, the Congress was impressive on account of its scope alone. Moreover, it enlarged the horizon of the non-Islamic participants as to the interrelation between religion and psychology as well as psychotherapy in Islamic countries, and that of the Islamic participants concerning the current state of secular psychology and psychotherapy compared to its state in the first part of the 20th century. The Congress demonstrated, amongst other things, that the Iranian clergy are willing and eager to work with researchers from other countries in the field of science and mental health; this at the outset of the third millennium and during the year of "Dialogue between Civilizations," and with mental health chosen for the first time by the World Health Organization as the theme for the 2001 Health Day ("Stop Exclusion, Dare to Care"). Also, given the rarity of publications on an Islamic approach to the field, the present article extends a report on the Congress proper by a corresponding analysis as well as comments and impressions by the non-Iranian authors. All authors were Congress participants.

In Western countries, the history and the present practice of psychology of religion as an academic discipline is largely based on theory and research developed within a Western, Judeo-Christian culture. In Islamic countries, an Islamic psychology and psychotherapy also has a long tradition. Unlike natural sciences such as physics or chemistry, which are based on natural laws recognized worldwide, psychology of religion deals with people of rather different cultures, attitudes, and degree of religiousness. Therefore, it is debatable to what extent, in psychology of religion, theories and findings from one particular culture can claim universal validity, even if they prove helpful in the original setting. If psychology of religion wants to become an international discipline recognized by all researchers in the field, whatever their location and religion, then these issues need to be clarified and discussed. In other words, one has to avoid both simply assuming the universal validity of a given approach and refusing to enter the discussion because one does not see its necessity or its potential fruitfulness.

We seize the occasion of the Tehran Congress to look from different cultural viewpoints at issues in religion and mental health, in religion and psychotherapy, and in epistemology. One aim is to raise everyone's consciousness of these issues (cf. Reich, 2002). This was already on our minds before the events of September 11, 2001. These events and their sequel have added weight to our advocacy for a dialogue, between representatives of various cultures, about the scientific issues in question. A further attempt in this direction is made in a companion article (Murken & Shah, this issue).

ABDOLVAHAB VAHABZADEH AND SHIVA KHALILI: PURPOSE AND SCOPE OF THE CONGRESS

Abdolvahab Vahabzadeh: The basic situation of dealing with mental health in the Eastern Mediterranean region was recently described by Dr. Ahmad Mohit

(2001), who also spoke at the Congress. He explicated notably that a more comprehensive approach to mental health, illness, and psychiatry was needed, an approach capable of understanding the bio-psycho-social, spiritual, historical, and even mythological aspects of human beings. To that effect, he said:

> religious leaders, intellectuals, women and men of conscience, thought and wisdom, government officials, parliamentarians and the like should be made aware of the importance of mental health and invited to assist in the development of better, more efficient and affordable systems of care. One thing is certain: it would not be possible to meaningfully improve the condition of mental health and the mentally ill without the involvement of all. (Mohit, 2001, p. 7)

This trend also characterizes the situation in Iran. In December 1998, The Office of Islamic Studies of the Tehran Psychiatric Institute, in collaboration with the University Leadership Office, held the First National Conference on Religion and Mental Health. This conference attempted to bring together scholars from both modern universities and traditional Islamic schools specializing in the conference topics (Ehsanmanesh & Karimi, 1999). The Islamization of psychology (and other disciplines) and of social life had been on the agenda of a number of scholars in Iran for the last 20 years (Hosseini, 1988). I attended the 1998 conference, and about the same time gave an invited lecture on stress (e.g., Vahabzadeh, 1999) to a small audience of neurologists. As I was educated partly in English academic institutions (i.e., London and Oxford), I first presented reductionistic empirical data, and then a more holistic, religious view. The audience was amazed by the latter, because most were of the opinion that neuroscience is centered on a surgical blade, and moreover that theology and science each have their specific realm with a clear separation between the two (cf. Al-Haddad, Shooka, & Raees, 1998; Lewis & Joseph, 1994; Majoub & Abdol Hafez, 1991; Maltby, McCollam, & Millan, 1994). On the contrary, for me, an Iranian Muslim by heritage, there exists no separation, let alone any dissonance between theology and science as I practice it in my profession (cf. Gartner, Hermatze, Hohmann, & Larson, 1990; Steeky, 1993). From such a perspective, it is crucial that both fields are represented in psychology, psychiatry, and neuroscience. This is so for reasons having to do both with maintaining the mental health of the present adult population of our country, and with the education of the next generation regarding healthy behavior.

Shiva Khalili: After the Islamic Revolution in Iran in 1979, one of the basic themes was "cultural revolution" focused on academic activities and universities. A main program of this cultural revolution was to review the relationship between Islam and the sciences in general and humanities in particular. During the past 22 years that relationship has been studied by many Iranian scientists, researchers, scholars, and thinkers. A special center was founded, the Office for the Cooperation of Howsa [Islamic Center] and the Universities; the Office has published numerous books and papers on this theme. Despite the efforts of this and similar centers, the universities and academies in Iran have stayed chiefly under the influence of the Western academic sciences.

The secular academic sciences have established themselves worldwide. However, in the last decades of the 20th century, we have witnessed many movements in Western countries and elsewhere aimed to maintain a dialogue between these academic sciences and religion. This trend was facilitated by a wider recognition of the implications of quantum mechanics, relativity theory, and recent philosophy of science as well as a turn to spirituality. New perspectives were also adopted in the fields of psychology, psychotherapy and mental health. However, because there is no homogeneous state of affairs in these fields, a wide spectrum of approaches toward religion and spirituality exists, many with a different foundation and with differing methods and goals (Khalili, 2001).

Unfortunately, a marked lack of information about these movements and recent achievements can be observed in most of the Islamic countries including among Iranian students, scholars, and the general public. Conversely, there are a sizeable number of individuals in Iran and other Islamic countries who have been working in the area of psychology and religion without getting the appropriate national and/or international attention or support. As the result, the absence of Islamic scientists and scholars can be observed in the international research community.

The efforts of the Department for Religious Studies, The Tehran Psychiatric Institute and those of Dr. Jafar Bolhari and his colleagues to organize an International Congress on Mental Health and Religion in 2001 were partly motivated by the wish to ameliorate the unsatisfactory situation just indicated.

Abdolvahab Vahabzadeh: When the Iranian Ministry of Health and Medical Education decided, at the request of the Iranian University of Medical Science (IUMS), to organize The First International Congress on Religion and Mental Health (in collaboration with the World Health Organization), I did my best to bring the Congress to international attention, this in a spirit of learning from each other (Wales, 1993) and getting to know each other better (Annan, 1999). As Director of the International Scientific Committee nominated by the Tehran Psychiatric Institute and the UN World Health Organization, I established worldwide contacts with colleagues and interested organizations. The issue of religion and mental health was to be opened up to researchers from different countries, cultures, and religions in a non-political, scientific, safe environment. I believe that thanks to a 2-year effort by the Committee, the staff, and myself, we had some measure of success in reaching that objective. My only regret is that there were not more non-Iranian scholars who participated—whether due to, even with my all-out assurances, some apprehensions about coming to Iran, or because the dates of the Congress were inconvenient because they fell on Easter, a major Christian celebration (not marked in the Islamic calendar).

From meeting delegates at the airport to the conference sessions and their breaks, through the meals and excursions and until the final good-bye, enriching discussions took place in which gray was an accepted color (besides black and white) and in which tolerance, honesty, dignity, and enthusiasm were present in addition to professional knowledge. However, to bear fruit, we need to evolve a common language both nationally and internationally. This will become possible if we continue along the lines traced at the Congress and in this publication.

SHIVA KHALILI: THE CONGRESS IN NUMBERS

The first work for organizing the Congress started at early 1999, both at the national and the international level: contacting individuals, organizations, and universities interested in or engaged with the subject of "Religion and mental health;" 78 WHO centers in various countries and about 204 centers and universities all over the world were contacted, from Azerbaijan to the United States. A special web site was designed and information material about the Congress was sent to individuals and organizations on request. As a result, we had more than 120 international responses. Forty of the respondents (from 15 different countries: Azerbaijan, Bangladesh, Brazil, Egypt, Germany, India, Italy, Malaysia, Morocco, The Netherlands, Pakistan, Russia, Switzerland, United Kingdom, United States) participated in the Congress with oral presentation or posters, and one from the Ukraine without a presentation.

Of the 242 (national and international) papers received by the Congress Secretary, 158 papers were selected for presentation at the Razi Conference Center of the Iranian University of Medical Sciences in Tehran: 70 papers to be presented in the Main Hall in Persian (Farsi) and English, and 60 in Hall 2 (in one language only); in addition there were 28 posters and one workshop (cf. Bolhari, 2001). All presentations, except one paper about new achievements in Neurosciences, focused on the central conference theme: Religion (mainly Judaism, Christianity, and Islam but also Zoroastrianism and Buddhism) and Mental Health. Research on a wide range of issues was reported; they can be classified under one or more of the following headings:

1. The role of religion and spirituality in primary prevention and promotion of mental health.
2. Religious ceremonies, prayer, meditation and mental health.
3. Stress and religious coping methods.
4. Psychotherapy, counseling and psycho-social rehabilitation using religious therapy.
5. The incidence and prevalence of drug abuse and suicide among religious populations.

6. Successful religious intervention for preventing drug abuse and HIV/Aids.
7. Clinical application of religious teachings.
8. Religion and mental disorders.
9. Research methodology in the field of religion, ethics and spirituality.
10. Religion and new achievements in neuroscience.
11. Common views of major religions regarding mental health issues.
12. New theories in the field of psychology, personality and religion.
13. Socio-cultural and psychological studies of religious populations.

Many papers presented empirical research; the first day of the conference was dedicated to the papers on theory and methodology. On the one hand, a number of researchers attempted to explain religion within naturalistic-scientific constructs from mainstream psychology and considered religion to be merely a resource for coping. On the other hand, many (national and international) researchers emphasized the possibility of a theistic psychology and presented their attempts to integrate psychology and religion more explicitly and completely. There is a hope that through such international conferences psychologists and psychotherapists engaged worldwide with religion and mental health will be encouraged to develop result-based theories and research methods and exchange views and experiences, leading toward a theoretical advance of psychology in general and religious psychology and psychology of religion in particular.

ASHIQ ALI SHAH: ISLAMIC PSYCHOLOGY OF RELIGION AND PSYCHOTHERAPY

The First International Congress on Religion and Mental Health was timely in view of the increasing scientific recognition of the impact of religion on the lives of people around the world. Once regarded as a form of neurosis by the Freudians (Freud, 1930/1962), and as unscientific by the Skinnerians because religion dealt with unobservable entities, religion is now accepted by mainstream psychology as an important aspect of people's lives. The 1992 American Psychological Association (APA) code of conduct acknowledges the role of religion in psychological services and the 4th edition of *Diagnostic and Statistical Manual (DSM–IV)* of the American Psychiatric Association includes a category on religious problems.

Contributions of Islamic Scholars to the Field

The influence of Islam as a religion and way of life in shaping the psychological and socio-cultural aspects of Muslims' lives was prominent since the times of the Prophet (SAW[1]). This encompassing Islamic conceptualization provided the foundations for

---

[1]SAW [or SAAS/SAWS]; Salla Allahu 'Alaihi Wa Sallam: May the blessing and the peace of Allah be upon him; English abbr.: Pbuh.

the meticulous work of early Muslim scientists, starting from the 7th century, in the fields of medicine, chemistry, mathematics, geography, astronomy, sociology, psychophysics, psychiatry, and psychotherapy. Before the dawn of the modern era of psychology, Muslim philosophers and thinkers elaborated on the causes of psychological problems and their treatment from an Islamic perspective. Contemporary Muslim psychologists have highlighted Ibn al-Haytham's (965–c.1040 CE) contributions to experimental psychology and psychophysics made before Bacon and Fechner (Khaleefa, 1999). The contribution of Ibn Sina (Avicenna; 980–1037 CE) to medicine and psychology on the subject of associative learning in adaptive and maladaptive responses was developed further by Al-Ghazali (1058–1128 CE). Al-Ghazali's theory of dynamic interaction deals with human emotions and their control, and he showed that ethical and emotional habits can be acquired and changed by learning and training. Ibn al-Qayyim (1981; 1292–1350 CE) stated in his book *Al-Fawa'id* that every action of a human person starts first as an inner thought or concealed speech or internal dialogue called *Khwatir* in Arabic. The prominent Muslim thinker Abu-Zaid al-Balkhi (1998; d. 934 CE) differentiated between neuroses and psychoses and classified neuroses into four categories, namely

1. Fear and anxiety.
2. Anger and aggression.
3. Sadness and depression.
4. Obsessions.

He outlined techniques how to preserve one's mental health. Almost all of the early Muslim philosophers regarded the balance between the needs of the physical self (*nafs*) and the spiritual self (*ruh*) as important to mental health.

Islamic Approach to Psychology

The Islamic approach to psychology focuses upon the Islamic principles and moral code of life as described in the Qur'an (the Revealed Book) and the Sunnah (the Sayings of the Prophet, SAW), and aims to achieve a balance (equilibrium) between the worldly and spiritual needs. This is considered to be a prerequisite for a balanced personality and mental health. Unlike a secular Western approach to psychology of religion that examines the variables of religious behavior or antecedents of religiosity, the Islamic approach to psychology examines and explains human mental processes, personality, and behaviors from an Islamic perspective; it is a religious psychology. Consequently, it borrows psychological constructs from the previously-mentioned two sources of guidance (i.e., Qur'an and Sunnah). Because practical knowledge for studying human behavior is usually derived from a general conceptual framework concerning human nature and its functioning, the Islamic approach to understanding human nature considers *Fitrah* as the elementary and central construct to explain human nature.

Fitrah and Human Nature

The Islamic view of human nature rests on the original purity and goodness of human beings, which is Fitrah. Fitrah is common to two basic constituents of human beings; *ruh* (soul, a transcendental self) and the *nafs* (physical or phenomenal self). Other views of Fitrah include Shah Wali Ullah's (2001; 1707–1762 CE) holistic conceptualization and Mohamed's (1998) integrated view of Fitrah related to the internal and external world of human beings, respectively. The former regards the spiritual as well as the biological components of humans as intrinsically good. According to this view, Fitrah includes both spiritual and physical tendencies that seek gratification in order to promote and achieve wholeness of a person's spiritual and physical constitution. The latter view relates Fitrah to a person's innate givens, but associates it also with human beliefs, values, attitudes, and views of the phenomenal world.

Fitrah is regarded as primordial faith which Allah (SWT[2]) Himself implanted into human nature (Mohamed, 1998). Fitrah implies submission to the will of Allah (SWT) and is the basis for *Tawhid* (Oneness of Allah: "There is no deity but Allah"). Many scholars believe that Fitrah is a state of intrinsic goodness. In Al-Qayyim's (1993–1997) view, Fitrah is truly an inborn predisposition to acknowledge Allah (SWT), *tawhid* and *din al-Islam*. Islamic faith is a life of obedience and submission to Allah. Imam an-Nawawi (1233–1273 CE) has defined Fitrah as the unconfirmed state of *Iman* (absolute belief) before individuals consciously affirms their belief.

Psychological Implication of Fitrah

The Islamic view of human beings based on Fitrah considers human activity or behavior as consciously determined. A behavior is regarded as a function of both the physical environment and the spiritual base. This makes the Islamic view of human nature a holistic one, as it integrates the physical and the psychical aspects with the spiritual aspect. According to Mohamed (1998), a person's control of the worldly tendencies of *nafs*, and the spiritual tendencies of *ruh*, establishes a healthy psycho-spiritual equilibrium. This can be achieved by consciously obeying the Divine commands and laws. The result tends toward the attainment of ultimate reality in the sense of self-realization, that is, the "attainment of the highest" as it was called by al-Ghazali (1979).

Furthermore, the Islamic approach to human nature regards values as an integral part of one's constitution. The human tendency to have values is inbuilt and their actual development depends upon events and conditions in the phenomenal world as well as in the metaphysical reality. Values are an important clue to a per-

---

[2]SWT; Subhanahu Wa Ta 'ala: Allah is purified of having partners or a son.

son's adherence to or deviation from Fitrah. Values, such as justice, mercy, patience, sacrifice, obedience, generosity, helpfulness, forgiveness, trust and so forth, constitute the character of an individual and his or her relationship with his or her Creator and the society.

The Islamic religious, moral, and social values are in accordance with the teachings of Qur'an and Sunnah, and hence, in my view, can be regarded as objectively defined—a view which may conceivably not be generally shared by secular psychologists. These values prescribe the moral and social code of conduct at the individual as well as at the collective levels. Whether one agrees or disagrees with them, or whether one conforms to or violates them, their normativity remains unaffected. Presumably, secular psychologists need to see data that show the beneficial effect of these values on mental and physical health.

Islamic Approach to Clinical Psychology and Psychotherapy

To emphasize a previous point, a proper control and transformation of *nafs* into the spiritual qualities of *ruh* is a pre-requisite for the healthy psycho-spiritual functioning of the individual. Al-Balkhi (1998) highlighted rational and spiritual methods to treat the different neuroses mentioned above. His book titled *Masalih al-Abdan wa'l-Anfus* (translation: *The Sustenance of Body and Soul*) contains the clinical and psychotherapeutic approaches to treating psychological problems. The various chapters deal with the following issues:

1. The importance of sustaining the health of the *nafs* via the soul (al-Balkhi's synonym for mind or psyche).
2. Mental hygiene or preventive mental health.
3. Regaining one's mental health if lost.
4. Psychological symptoms and their classification.
5. Management of anger and getting rid of its symptoms.
6. Ways to tranquilize fear and panic.
7. How to get rid of sadness and severe depression.
8. Ways of fighting obsessions and the harmful inner speech of the *nafs*.

Al-Balkhi stated that helping people with their psychological symptoms is more important when compared to dealing with their physical symptoms. A person may live for years without complaining from a physical symptom but psychological symptoms are bedeviling us all the time. He suggested, therefore, that just as healthy people keep some drugs and first aid medicines nearby for unexpected physical emergencies, they should also keep healthy thoughts and feelings in their minds for unexpected emotional outbursts. There are number of other early Muslim philosophers, such as Ibni Sina, Ibnil Haitham, Al-Razi, Ibni Aqayyim, Miskaweh, to mention just a few, who have not only listed and discussed psychological disorders but also their treatment labeled *al-ilaj annafsani* (psychological treatment or psychotherapy) or *al-ilaj bildhid* (reciprocal inhibition). The contemporary Muslim psychologists are in process of reviving the traditions of their predecessors by instilling earlier insight into the discipline of psychology. The contributions include Achoui (1998), Ajmal (1986), Ansari (1992), Badri (1976, 1978, 1996), Mohamed (1995, 1998), and Shah (1996, 2001). I now attempt to outline psychotherapy in the Islamic context.

The Islamic psychotherapeutic approach emphasizes the biological, social, and spiritual aspects of individuals. It considers their spiritual aspect as well as their values in adjusting within society. This approach regards the egoistic and individualistic concerns of a person and confusion about social and religious values as one of the major causes of psychological problems. The problem of the client is handled with reference to the society. Any attempt within the Islamic approach to exclude values and to conduct psychotherapy without considering the socio-religious circumstances of the client would be regarded as an exercise in futility.

The psychologist analyses the problem of the client and also tries to find out, with the client, the solution of the problem in accordance with the social and religious guidelines. In this regard the psychotherapist acts as a guide and reformer for the individual. The practice of Islamic psychotherapy requires the therapist to be well versed in the Islamic tradition and to be a practicing Muslim in letter and spirit. Psychotherapists should regard it as their professional and moral duty to remove the confusion in their clients about social and moral values and to enable them to perceive their problems within this context. Thus, Muslim psychotherapists adhering to these values "reflect" them rather than impose any of their own on the client. The experience of the author as a psychotherapist shows that the clients do not dispute these values, they do not feel themselves misunderstood, and they do not complain if the therapist adheres to these values in psychotherapy.

Islamic psychotherapy is reflective, directive, and critically supportive. Psychotherapists not only analyze the feelings of the client but also are active and suggest to clients the steps and actions essential for their improvement. The focus of the psychotherapy is on the present problem, rather than exploring the unconscious dynamics of the client. However, clients are assisted and helped to learn from the mistakes of the past and to look to the future with determination to bring about positive change in their lifestyles. Other authors describe Islamic psychotherapy as prescriptive and future oriented (Mohamed, 1995), which is consistent with ideas presented here.

In Islamic psychotherapy the thoughts and actions of a client that are incongruent with the basic Islamic tenets are thoroughly analyzed. The emphasis of the therapy is on the religious and cultural values. Although the therapy is taking place in a dyadic context, continuous reference is made to the society and interpersonal relationships. This emphasis stresses the importance and beneficial effects of the family and social bonds over against all-out individualism and selfish concerns. The therapy is directed toward self-realization in terms of self-knowledge as a moral principle. This can be achieved through the exercise of restraint and control in the sense of voluntary simplicity. In the opinion I represent, materialistic and sexual needs are transitory, unstable, and repetitive (Shah, 1996). The pursuit of these needs does not lead to a real satisfaction; rather it stimulates these desires endlessly. Hence, the client is encouraged to give up the materialistic, selfish, and asocial desires in the spirit of the Islamic virtue of self-restraint or contention. The clients are helped and supported to view their relationship with others on a give-and-take basis, that is in the framework of Haqooq-ul-Ibad (the revealed rights of fellow human beings). Clients try to understand their weakness and to change their outlook of the social world around them.

SEBASTIAN MURKEN: SOME SUBSTANTIVE ISSUES IN THE CONGRESS

The Tehran International Congress on Religion and Mental Health not only covered an important subject but also one that draws more and more attention in Western countries as shown, for instance, by the founding of the journal *Mental Health, Religion and Culture* in 1998. Like others, I am thankful and feel honored that I was able to attend the conference as one of the few Europeans and as the only participant from Germany. My invited response to the Congress comes under five headings:

1. The need for and value of academic discourse.
2. Epistemology.
3. Methodological issues.
4. Content of the studies presented.
5. Outlook for the future.

Academic Discourse

The time frame of the Congress was quite ambitious. Usually, seven papers of 15 minutes each were presented in a 2-hour time block, with the remaining 15-minute slot used for a general discussion. However, usually there were no discussions because of the accumulated overrunning of the time allocated to the presentations. This was regrettable for two reasons. First, one would have liked to inquire about details concerning the instruments used, the sample, or any specific problem encountered in the conduct of the study, and so on. Second, progress in scientific knowledge can only be acquired if we ask each other and ourselves critical questions. Debating competently differing views will lead to new insights and progress. Therefore, in the closing session others and I suggested providing more discussion time in the paper sessions and inviting respondents for the main lectures.

Epistemological Assumptions and Issues

In 1987, I happened to participate in the Islamic World Conference on Religion and Mental Health in Cairo. I attended one of the scientific sessions in which two researchers from the United States and from Pakistan, respectively, presented their papers. After some listening, I realized that these scientists, though speaking about the same topic, namely religion and mental health, did so on the basis of quite different epistemological assumptions.

For the researcher from the United States, it was simply choosing sets of variables (religion being one of them), getting the data, and working out the statistics. For the researcher from Pakistan, religion seemed to be the very foundation of his scientific inquiry. The puzzling phenomenon was that nobody seemed to notice these epistemological differences in the basic assumptions of their scientific inquiries. These differences were unnoticed, or at least unexpressed. Since that time, I am intrigued that we take our cultural presuppositions so much for granted, and I am amazed how difficult it is to ask critical questions about possible cultural biases. Consequently, the invitation to the Tehran Congress was a welcome opportunity for me and other non-Iranian participants to learn more about the relation between culture and science. It was an opportunity to become more conscious about one's own underlying scientific assumptions and to engage in a dialogue with scientists doing research from an Islamic religious perspective.

What several non-Iranian visitors experienced during the Congress and in many private discussions was indeed a difference of "scientific cultures." To make this obvious, I here put side by side a Western secularized perspective and an Islamic religious perspective of scientific research as they were presented at the Congress and then draw some conclusions. Note, however, that there also exist Western authors, for example Dale E. Matthews, who make psychological claims from a (Christian) religious perspective. A secular model of Western epistemology, that is a mainstream, evidence-based, Western understanding of the psychology of religion, is shown in Figure 1. Modern sociology understands society as the result of interacting subsystems each with its own structure and internal logic. Some of the major subsystems are shown in Figure 1: economics, politics, science, and religion being some among other subsystems making up society. Religion, then, has no privileged position.

The question that comes to mind immediately is the following: How does social science in Western society deal with the truth claims of religion, or better, with the truth claims of different religions? For the psychology of religion, as distinct from

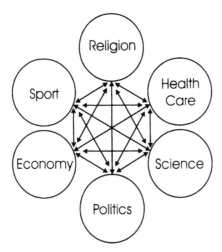

FIGURE 1   A secular model of Western epistemology.

a religious or theological psychology, the answer is clear: The truth claims of reli-gions are not matters of scientific inquiry. This principle of the exclusion of the truth claims about the nature of the Transcendent (God) is a guideline for the psy-chology of religion since Theodore Flournoy (1903) formulated it a century ago. What does it mean? From Flournoy's perspective, the task of the researcher is to understand how the Transcendent is perceived and dealt with by the person stud-ied, not to research whether the Transcendent exists or what its attributes could be. In the understanding of its practitioners, this is not a reductionistic perspective but a necessary psychological self-restriction in order to be able to deal with different truth claims in a society rather than making judgments about religious truth claims. Consequently, from a completely secularized perspective, explanations about the efficacy of religion concerning mental health must be based exclusively on psy-chological theories and must be researched using genuinely empirical methods.

What happens if we take a different perspective? Figure 2 shows a model of re-ligion-based epistemology as it was encountered in many of the Islamic religious contributions. Religion, then, is not one cultural subsystem among others but the basis and framework of everything else (cf. the previous section "Islamic Ap-proach to Psychology" by A. A. Shah, and its sequels). It is a primary, non-reduc-ible phenomenon.

Such an epistemological option has been adopted by Islamic scholars and, as previ-ously indicated, by some Western Christian writers. Matthews and Clark (1998), authors of *The Faith Factor,* explained in the introduction to this book that "I have learned to be-lieve that God does heal" (p. 11). Seen from such a perspective, which implies the inclu-sion of transcendence, the scientific process and the understanding of the phenomena are

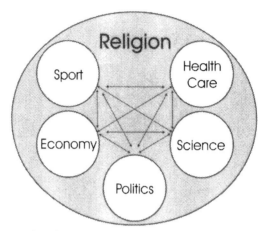

FIGURE 2   Model of a religion-based epistemology.

quite different. Now, not only natural, psychological explanations, but also supernatural, that is transcendent explanations, have to be considered.

When comparing the two epistemological approaches illustrated in Figures 1 and 2, two major sets of considerations arise. First, both of the approaches are models and are culturally bound. The purely naturalistic model with its claim to exclude the truth claims of supernatural causality is, from the perspective of the second, religious model, not value neutral but is itself equally a model with a truth claim. The implicit truth claim of the first model is that the appropriate level of analysis for a scientific psychological explanation is the naturalistic level, not the supernatural level. In other words, God may or may not intervene, but as a science, psychology approaches the study of religious belief, behavior, feelings, and so forth in the same way that it approaches the study of all human behavior, on the assumption that there are regularities that can be understood and formulated and put in the form of a theory. The tantalizing question is whether these differing models with their different assumptions can be fruitfully contrasted and compared, and their cultural, religious, and psychological "bias" be reflected and communicated.

Second, the data taken and their interpretation may differ. Research based on the first model might ignore transcendent aspects and explanations. Using the second model might lead one to ignore a wider range of psychological processes and explanations. The question is: How can data collected in different countries by researchers with different backgrounds and epistemologies be compared and interpreted?

In principle, one option would be to find a metasystem or language that is capable of integrating the two differing perspectives. At present, however, it is not clear what this metasystem could look like. It seems more modest and more feasible to construct a bridge that can be accessed from either side (cf. Reich, 2000).

To ask the same questions of people living in different cultures and having different religions seems a promising way to understand cultural biases and to work through them, providing that it is done in a mutually agreed way. From such a perspective the Tehran Congress was an important starting point for an encounter of professionals from many cultures and countries. It is increasingly necessary to deepen and enrich our mutual understanding and the understanding of religion as a major element in people's lives.

Contents of the Studies Presented

Many of the studies presented at the Congress correlate just one set of variables (religion) with another set of variables (mental health) and find certain correlation coefficient values. I suggest some caution as to the significance of the effect of religion thus determined. As far as I know the literature, the largest positive effects of religiosity hardly ever explain more than 5 or 6 % of variance of the mental health criteria. To understand the place of mental health in people's lives, it is therefore important to include other relevant variables like physical health status, socio- economic status, self-esteem, social support system and so on. If we understand mental disorders exclusively in religious terms, for example as a punishment for the non-observation of religious laws, we might miss important alternative social and psychological explanations, for instance those proposed for the world-wide problem of increasing depression (Murken, 1998).

Outlook for the Future

The particular importance of the Tehran Congress lies in the coming together of scholars of religion and mental health from all over the world. It would be most promising to continue the energy and spirit of this Congress to the point of designing novel studies that include groups of people from different cultures and religions (for both subject samples and researchers) as done by Furnham and Baguma (1999). The psychology of religion in Western countries involves mostly a Western and predominantly Christianized population. In Islamic countries, the perspective is determined by the Qur'an and the Sunnah. The study of religion and religiosity needs to expand its scope from a "local" to a worldwide cooperative enterprise in which scholars learn from each other through the process, and through which they become adept at looking at a particular research project from different perspectives of all kinds (cf. Ghorbani, Watson, Ghramaleki, Morris, & Hood, 2000; Hansen, 1998; Ineichen, 1998).

K. HELMUT REICH: COMPARING THE
TEHRAN CONGRESS WITH SIMILAR
CONFERENCES ELSEWHERE

Whereas largely agreeing with Sebastian Murken's remarks, yet emphasizing the specificity of the religious domain (see, e.g., papers by Edwards & Lowis, Schoenrade, Hay, & Boyatzis, in Paloutzian, 2001; Reich, 2000, 2001), I would like to add the following observations. The scope and participation of the conference were most impressive (Bolhari, 2001). At the (formally) comparable 2001 Annual APA Convention in San Francisco, 55 papers by 135 authors and 33 posters by about 100 authors were presented in the sessions organized by APA Division 36 (Psychology of Religion; Krejci, 2001), of which 20 papers by 50 authors and 20 posters by about 70 authors concerned religion and mental health (classed "generously"). Accepting that these numbers are approximate, the scope of the Tehran Congress nevertheless stands out in comparison. More importantly, religion and mental health are well-represented research topics in either setting. Clearly, the importance of religiosity for almost all aspects of life but also for psychology and psychotherapy is increasingly recognized by science. In the West, secular psychology of religion is only about 100 years old, and most research was and is done "locally," with Christians and Jews as research subjects. Correspondingly, researchers in Iran study those who hold the Muslim faith, because it happens to be Muslims who are there. The present Congress therefore was a good opportunity to widen one's horizons and get answers to the following questions: What is the relation between Islam, psychology, and psychotherapy? What are the empirical results obtained by Islamic researchers? And so on.

For both Sebastian Murken and myself, the more intuitive notions of psychology and religion (or even religious psychology) and psychology of religion were clarified and detailed after reading Ashiq Ali Shah's earlier explications. Let us not forget, however, that such a version of research has its place in Western countries too, as exemplified by a number of papers in the *Journal of Psychology and Christianity* and similar publications. And if somebody is surprised by a publication titled "Mental Health in the Verses of Holy Qur'an for Mental Health and School Staff," he or she should be aware of international conferences such as "Psychological Aspects of Biblical Concepts of Persons," Free University of Amsterdam, The Netherlands, 4-6 March, 2002.

I would not like to conclude without emphasizing my full agreement with Ashiq Ali Shah's and Sebastian Murken's well-deserved praise of the friendliness of our hosts, the excellence of the facilities and, in particular, the outstanding quality of the translations, all of which contributed considerably to making the Congress such a memorable experience. Last, but certainly not least (given the restrictions of women's activities under the Taliban regime in neighboring Afghanistan), let me record how impressed I was by the visible participation and the activities of the recently established Research Institute for the Rehabilitation and Improvement of Women's Life as well as by the competence and assurance of the women speakers at the conference.

ASHIQ ALI SHAH: THE CONGRESS ITSELF

The Congress attracted a large number of participants from all over the world. The delegates belonged to different professions, including academics from universities, professionals from the field of psychology, psychiatry and general medicine, clergymen, priests, social workers, and members of non-governmental organizations (NGOs). They shared their knowledge about religion and mental health based on their research and experience in the field. Although the approaches of these papers were diverse, the growing understanding of the influence of religion in people's lives and its positive impact on the health of the individual was common among all. The papers presented by the Muslim scholars, but also by some Western scholars, underscored the importance of spirituality in the mental health of individuals. A large number of papers by the scholars of the host country indicated the role of spirituality in the mental health of Iranians.

The significance of this conference for the host country could be understood from the extent of its media coverage by the state-owned as well as private mass media. The reporters of Iran television, as well as of national newspapers, daily interviewed foreign and local delegates about the conference activities and the issues pertaining to religion and mental health. Iranian television also recorded roundtable discussions about the issues discussed at the Congress and the growing impact of religion and mental health. The peak of the media coverage of the conference was a live talk show organized by the Iranian television, in its program *Pertau*, to discuss the current issues related to religion and mental health in the developing and developed countries. One local and two foreign delegates were invited to highlight the role of religion in mental health, especially the incidence of depression among the religious and nonreligious people. The discussants took the view that spiritual orientation of people had an immunizing effect against the psychological illnesses.

The academic program of the conference, lodging and boarding, conference material, guidance and help, if needed, were meticulous. The arrangements for simultaneous translation, from Persian to English and vice versa, were well maintained throughout the four days of the conference. Murken mentioned already the suggestion made at the closing panel session that in the future some time should be given to discussions, and a proper time slot for the poster presentations provided. As to his remarks on epistemology, contents of the studies presented, and outlook for the future, my views have been set out in the foregoing section on Islamic psychology of religion and psychotherapy, and are elaborated further in the companion article (Murken & Shah, this issue).

The hosts conspicuously displayed the traditional hospitality, warmth, and friendliness of Islamic culture on all the occasions throughout the conference. The pick-up and drop-off service from the airport and to and from the conference venue and the hotel, the care-taking guides, the comfortable accommodations, and plenty of delicious food served during the conference were the hallmark of this hospitality. I have missed some of these things at conferences elsewhere. On top of this, there were daily excursions and shopping tours at the end of the conference's daily sessions. I was amazed about the self-sufficiency of the Iranians despite sanctions by the United States. Although the economic conditions of Iran are not as booming as they were during the 1970s and 1980s, it was impressive how they have kept their economy going under adverse circumstances.

Mehdi Karroubi, the honorable speaker of the Iranian parliament, graced the closing ceremony of the conference, which underscored its significance. The end of the conference was a welcome occasion to participate in the hosts' organized tours to the historic and ancient cities of Shiraz and Persepolis, and to Isfahan.

BRIEF OVERALL IMPRESSIONS FROM IRAN

K. Helmut Reich

What strikes one most in Tehran (apart from the specificity of the road traffic)? The hillside topology, the boulevards and squares, the parks, the museums showing the millenary-old, rich cultural heritage, and other commonalities? Or the dress code for women (also to be adopted by tourists, though possibly less strictly), the gender separation in public places (buses, entrance to airports, mausoleums, etc.), the taboo against a woman shaking hands with a man not belonging to her family? Clearly, "what goes without saying" is not necessarily the same in Iran and in Western countries.

Short-term visitors, the boulevard press, and even some scientific studies have a tendency to paint things in black and white, to dichotomize observations. However, Iran is a complex country and culture that needs to be known in all its diversity. Iranians understand that most human beings need poetry as much as physics, theology as much as theories, music as much as mathematics. Thus, there are not only beautiful birds in public birdhouses, unique historical landmarks such as Persepolis, marvelous places of remembrance of great poets and the like, but Iran also participates in the research activities of the European Laboratory for Particle Research at Geneva, Switzerland, and other projects.

What about the Shari'ah, the law of Islam, based upon the Qur'an, the Sunna, parallel traditions and work of Muslim scholars in the two first centuries of Islam? A recent article (Tamandonfar, 2001) detailed its workings in Iran. Unfortunately, this article—welcome *per se*—says little about the reformers, about President Khatami and the popular support he has for carrying on with the reforms. Anyway, conversing with Iranians, one becomes aware of how much the system has been reformed already in the last years, compared to the early days of the Islamic Republic of Iran.

Sebastian Murken

The attendance of the Tehran Conference provided me with the opportunity to stay some extra days and to visit some more places and cities. What did impress me most? (a) The extraordinary friendliness of the people both toward visitors, but also to each other. The Iranian language seems to be full of very polite phrases and sayings, and people care for each other. (b) The dryness of this country. After a shortage of rain for several years now, Iran is mainly a desert. The problems resulting from this state of affairs are enormous, and draw attention to the value of water and the worldwide responsibility every country has for its economic consumption. (c) For me personally, the nightly climbing from Tehran (Darband – Namazi, 1999) to the mountain Towchal (3933m) of the Alborz range was certainly a strenuous highlight. (d) Like the other participants, I was moved and fascinated by the beautiful remains of the ancient cultures, and particularly the Islamic culture—the ruins of Bam, the old city of Yazd, Esfahan, and the Gardens of Shiraz.

A FINAL WORD FROM ALL AUTHORS

Thanks to The First International Congress on Religion and Mental Health in Tehran we had an opportunity to become aware and learn about a number of issues that previously we simply ignored or were not attentive to. We hope that a constructive dialogue will continue, providing an opportunity for all to learn more.

REFERENCES

Achoui, M. (1998). Human nature from a comparative psychological perspective. *The American Journal of Islamic Social Science, 15,* 71–95.

Ajmal, M. (1986). *Muslim contributions to psychotherapy and other essays.* Islamabad: National Institute of Psychology.

Al-Balkhi, A. Z. (1998). *Masalih al-Abdan wa 'l-Anfus* [Sustenance for body and soul] (Facsimile edition reproduced from MS Ayasofya 3740 Süleymaniye Library, Istanbul; F. Sezgin, Ed.). Frankfurt/Main, Germany: University Institute for the History of Arabic-Islamic Science, Publication 2a, Series C.

Al-Ghazali, A.-H. (n.d.). *Iha, Uloom Addeen* [Revival of religious sciences]. Beirut: Dar al-Qalam.

Al-Ghazali, M. (2001). *The socio-political thought of Shah Wali Ullah.* Islamabad: Islamic Research Institute Press.

Al-Ghazzali, A. -H. (1979). *Kimiya 'al-SA 'adah* [The alchemy of happiness] (C. Field, Trans.; 2nd ed.). Lahore: Sh. Muhammad Ashraf Publisher.

Al-Haddad, M. K., Shooka, A., & Raees, A. (1998). OCD in Bahrain: A phenomenological Profile. *Journal of Social Psychiatry, 44,* 143–145.

Al-Qayyim al-Jawziyyah, I. (1981). *Al-Faw. id* [The spiritual benefits]. Beirut: Dar al-Nafa, is.

Al-Qayyim al-Jawziyyah, I. (1993–1997). *Natural healing with the medicine of the Prophet* (S. M. al-Akili, Ed. & Trans.). Philadelphia, PA: Pearl.

Annan, K. (1999). *Dialogue of civilization and need for world ethic.* Oxford, England: Oxford Centre for Islamic Studies.

An-Nawawi, Y. S. -D. (n.d.). An-Nawawi's forty Hadiths (E. Ibrahim & D. Johnson-Davies, Trans.; The International Islamic Federation of Students Organizations ed.). Riyadh, Saudi Arabia: International Islamic Publishing House.

Ansari, Z. A. (Ed.). (1992). *Qur'anic concepts of human psyche.* Islamabad, Pakistan: International Institute of Islamic Thought.

Badri, M. B. (1976). *Islam and alcoholism.* Washington, DC: American Trust Publications.

Badri, M. B. (1978). *The dilemma of Muslim psychologists.* London: M.H.W. Publishers.

Badri, M. B. (1996). Counselling and psychotherapy from an Islamic perspective. *Al-Shajarah: Journal of the International Institute of Islamic Thought & Civilisation (ISTAC, Kuala Lumpur),* 1–240.

Bolhari, J. (Ed.). (2001). *Abstract book of The First International Congress of Religion and Mental Health, Tehran, 16-19 April 2001.* Tehran: Iranian University of Medical Sciences.

Ehsanmanesh, M. & Karimi, I. (1999). *Proceedings of the First Congress on Religion and Mental Health.* Ghom, Iran: Navid-e-Islam.

Flournoy, T. (1903) Les principes de la psychologie religieuse [Principles of psychology of religion]. *Archives de Psychologie, I,* 33–57.

Freud, S. (1962). *Civilization and its discontents.* New York: Norton. (Original work published 1930)

Furnham, A., & Baguma, P. (1999). Cross-cultural differences in explanations for health and illness: A British and Ugandan comparison. *Mental Health, Religion & Culture, 2,* 121–134.

Gartner, J., Hermatze, M., Hohmann, A., & Larson, D. (1990). The effect of patient and clinical ideology on clinical judgment. *Psychotherapy, 27,* 98–106.

Ghorbani, N., Watson, P. J., Ghramaleki, A. F., Morris, R. J., & Hood, R. W., Jr. (2000). Muslim attitudes towards religion scale: Factors, validity and complexity of relationships with mental health in Iran. *Mental Health, Religion & Culture, 3*(2), 125–132.

Hansen, C. (1998). Long-term effects of religious upbringing. *Mental Health, Religion & Culture, 1,* 91–112.

Hosseini, S. A. (1988). *The Islamic school of psychology.* Mashad, I.R. Iran: Ferdowsi University Press.

Ineichen, B. (1998). The influence of religion on the suicide rate: Islam and Hinduism compared. *Mental Health, Religion & Culture, 1,* 31–36.

Khaleefa, O. (1999). Who is the founder of psychophysics and experimental psychology? *The American Journal of Islamic Social Sciences, 16,* 1–26.

Khalili, S. (2001, April). *Towards psychological theories based on an Islamic approach: Comparison of non-religious schools of psychology and theistic schools of psychology.* Paper presented at The First International Congress on Religion and Mental Health, Tehran, University of Medical Sciences.

Krejci, M. J. (Ed.). (2001, Summer). 2001 Division 36 Convention Program for the 109th Annual Convention of the American Psychological Association. *Psychology of Religion Newsletter. American Psychological Association Division 36, 26*(3), 1–6.

Lewis, C. A., & Joseph, S. (1994). Obsessive actions and religious practices. *Journal of Psychology, 128,* 699–700.

Majoub, O. M., & Abdol Hafez, H. B. (1991). Pattern of OCD in Eastern Saudi Arabia. *British Journal of Psychiatry, 185,* 840–842.

Maltby, J., McCollam, P. & Millan, D. (1994). Religiosity and obsessionality. *Journal of Psychology, 128,* 609–611.

Matthews, D. A., & Clark, C. (1998). *The faith factor: Proof of the healing power of prayer* (Paperback ed.). New York: Penguin.

Mohamed, Y. (1995). Fitrah and its bearing on the principles of psychology. *The American Journal of Islamic Social Sciences, 12,* 1–18.

Mohamed, Y. (1998). *Human nature in Islam.* Kuala Lumpur: A. S. Noordeen.

Mohit, A. (2001). Psychiatry and mental health for developing countries, challenges for the 21st century. Retrieved June 26, 2002 from http://www.who.sci.eg/MNH/WHD/TechPres-Pakistan.pdf

Murken, S. (1998). *Gottesbeziehung und psychische Gesundheit. Die Entwicklung eines Modells und seine empirische Überprüfung* [God relationship and mental health. The development of a model and its empirical testing]. Münster, Germany: Waxmann.

Namazi, S. (April 21, 1999). Darband. *The Iranian* [Online]. Retrieved June 26, 2002 from http://www.iranian.com/SiamakNamazi/April99/Darband/index.html

Paloutzian, R. F. (Ed.). (2001). Invited essay and commentaries on the Batson-Schoenrade-Ventis model of religious experience: Contribution by A. C. Edwards & M. J. Lowis; and commentaries by P. Schoenrade, D. Hay, and C. H. Boyatzis. *The International Journal for the Psychology of Religion, 11,* 215–258.

Reich, K. H. (2000). Between the Scilla of the philosophy of scientific knowledge and the Charybdis of personal conviction and experience: Which course? *Journal of Psychology and Theology, 28*(3), 190–200.

Reich, K. H. (2001, April). *Spiritual Development.* Paper presented at The First International Congress on Religion and Mental Health, Tehran, University of Medical Sciences.

Reich, K. H. (2002). Developing the horizons of the mind: Relational and contextual reasoning and the resolution of cognitive conflicts. Cambridge, England: Cambridge University Press.

Shah, A. A. (1996, July). *Islamic approach to psychopathology and its treatment.* Paper presented at the National Seminar on Islamization of Psychology, Department of Psychology. Kuala Lumpur: International Islamic University Malaysia.

Shah, A. A. (2001, April). *Islamic therapeutic approach to mental health.* Paper presented at The First International Congress on Religion and Mental Health, Tehran, University of Medical Sciences.

Steeky G. (1993, July 2). *Treatment of obsessive-compulsive disorders.* New York: Guilford.

Tamandonfar, M. (2001). Islam, law, and political control in contemporary Iran. *Journal for the Scientific Study of Religion, 40,* 205–219.

Vahabzadeh, A. (1999). Studies on the role of insulin on behavioral and neuroendocranial indices of stress, using brain microdialysis in rats. *Journal of Iranian University of Medical Sciences, 6,* 153–161.

Wales, H. R. H. P. (1993). *Islam and the West.* Oxford, England: Oxford Centre for Islamic Studies.

THE INTERNATIONAL JOURNAL FOR THE PSYCHOLOGY OF RELIGION, *12*(4), 239–254

INVITED ESSAY

Naturalistic and Islamic Approaches to Psychology, Psychotherapy, and Religion: Metaphysical Assumptions and Methodology—A Discussion

Sebastian Murken
Center for Psychobiological and Psychosomatic Research
University of Trier, Germany

Ashiq Ali Shah
Department of Psychology
International Islamic University Malaysia, Kuala Lumpur

THE DISCUSSION

The present discussion arose from the work on the Tehran Congress Report (Khalili, Murken, Reich, Shah, & Vahabzadeh, this issue). Knowledge of that report is helpful for better understanding this exchange between the present two authors, especially Shah's exposition of Islamic psychology and psychotherapy. This article aims at presenting the two approaches, their commonalities and differences, and above all, the possibilities for collaboration despite these differences. The discussion begins with a long initial statement by each author. These are followed by a

Requests for reprints should be sent to Sebastian Murken, Psychology of Religion Research Group, Center for Psychobiological and Psychosomatic Research, University of Trier, Franziska-Puricelli-Str. 3, D-55543 Bad Kreuznach, Germany. E-mail: smurken@mainz-online.de. Or to, Ashiq Ali Shah, Department of Psychology, International Islamic University Malaysia, Kuala Lumpur, 53100 Jalan Gombak, Kuala Lumpur, Malaysia. E-mail: ashiq213@yahoo.com section that presents the remarks of both authors, formulated and interspersed after taking into account the responses of each author to the initial exchanges.

SEBASTIAN MURKEN: OPENING REMARKS

I have set out my basic views in my earlier report (Khalili et al., this issue). In a specifically naturalistic and secularized model of Western epistemology, society is conceived as being the result of interacting subsystems, each with its own structure and internal logic—for example, economics, politics, science, and religion (e.g., Luhmann, 1995). Religion, in this case, has no privileged position. In contrast, in a model of religion-based epistemology, religion is not one cultural subsystem among others but is instead the basis and framework of everything else, in particular, in the context of the present discussion, of doing research in Islamic psychology.

My intention is to propose a bridge that can be accessed from either side and that acknowledges either approach. Irrespective of culturally based truth claims, such a bridge could be constructed by formulating common scientific and methodological standards which could include the following:

1. If at all possible, studies should use a control group in their design in order to avoid hermeneutic circular reasoning in the sense of self-fulfilling prophecies.

2. Studies should be based on hypotheses that can be tested and thus potentially falsified. Without the formulation of hypotheses the theoretical understanding of phenomena remains limited. A statistical correlation is not a theory. And, to put it unambiguously: Theological doctrines are no falsifiable theories either.

3. When interpreting the results, one should be aware of one's own truth claims. It would be helpful to reflect these and to make them transparent.

To ask the same questions of people living in different cultures and having different religions seems to be a promising way to understand cultural biases and to work through them, providing that it is done as just outlined (e.g., Hood et al., 2001).

Epistemology

As a basis for discussion, here is a summary of the change in epistemology in the 20th century, as I understand it. Thanks to the work of Norwood Russell Hanson (1958, 1971), Karl Popper (1935, 1963, 1972), Thomas S. Kuhn (1970), Imre Lakatos (1970, 1978), Paul Feyerabend (1975, 1978, 1981), Larry Laudan (1990) and others, the conceptual foundations of science have undergone a marked change in the second part of the 20th century. Taking the cue from Helmut Reich (2002, pp. 35–37), I see this change as follows. The earlier classical realism rests on the assumptions that

(1) there is a reality independent of human ideas and theories; (2) scientific theories and the theoretical entities contained in them purport to refer to those real entities, processes, or structures existing independently of the theories; (3) hence, scientific theories can be judged to be true or false in some sense larger than merely that "they allow one to describe, predict, and organize the experimental data." The latter could be called "epistemic truth" whereas the former is "ontic truth." (Kitchener, 1988, p. 17)

Thus, the scientific theories assumed by classical realism involve ontic truth, not just the epistemic truth of theories "merely" aimed at describing, predicting, and organizing empirical data.

Foundationalism follows from the purported ontic truth of scientific theories. Laudan (1990) enumerates the resulting foundational epistemological program as

(1) a search for incorrigible givens from which the rest of knowledge could be derived; (2) a commitment to giving advice about how to improve knowledge; and (3) the identification of criteria for recognizing when one had a bona fide claim. (p. 134)

However, the impact of the work begun by Hanson (1958) has convinced most contemporary philosophers of scientific knowledge that foundationalism can no longer be justified (e.g., Laudan). Indeed, by now it has become clear that (a) all observations are theory-laden, i.e., influenced by pre-knowledge; (b) scientific theories are underdetermined by facts, for example, several theories may explain a given data set "equally well;" (c) verification or falsification of a theory is more complex than thought previously (the *experimentum crucis* is an exceptional occurrence); and (d) the underlying assumptive framework, perhaps unwittingly chosen, provides an influential hermeneutic context for one's research (cf. Lakoff & Johnson, 1999).

If this conceptualization is adopted, one can no longer refer to the only true and best theory, but one can still make comparisons according to the following criteria: The approach, model, or theory considered more effective, would—each time compared to its rival—(a) explain broader ranges of different kinds of phenomena, (b) have been tested in more areas, (c) already have led to more unexpected discoveries or applications, (d) yielded more precise results, (e) be more dependable, (f) possibly be the only candidate that offers a satisfactory explanation for certain phenomena. When making the comparison between the rivals, it is understood that no criterion from (a) to (f) is individually sufficient for a ranking but that all criteria count jointly for a preference, even though it can be changed later. In other words, the preferred approach, model, or theory wins a relative victory, not an absolute one; and in case the comparison is repeated after further work on a nonpreferred competitor, it may well become the dominant view. The basis and results of such comparisons can be agreed interindividually, and thereby gain scientific credence.

Methodological Issues

Science implies that we lack knowledge about certain things. The scientific process should be designed to make us more knowledgeable about questions so far unanswered. For this we eventually need a theory, not just correlational studies, which indicate the strength of a relationship between variables, but not the nature of that relationship. Scientific methodology demands that the testing itself leaves the result open. For instance, if one wants to explore the interrelation between religion and depression, a hypothesis could be about (a) religion-induced depression, such that thinking that everything is in God's hands makes one feel powerless and helpless, which might therefore sustain depression. One could test this by assessing religiosity, locus of control, and level of depression, and by then comparing the results with those from a control group. Another hypothesis could be about (b) religion-induced resilience, such that religion prevents depression through the possibility of referring problems to a Higher Power, which can be supportive within life's demands. This second hypothesis could be tested in a way similar to the first one. Constructing a theory built on either hypothesis, or on alternative ones, would be supported by whichever evidence is better. This is obviously not possible if the issue has been preempted by working with a single unfalsifiable assumption.

Many of the studies presented at the Tehran Congress and elsewhere in the field of Religion and Health lack a theory. For the most part they only explore associations between various measures of religiousness and mental health. I suggest some caution in interpreting the significance of the effect of religion on mental health determined in this way. As far as I know the literature, the largest positive effects of religiosity hardly ever explain more than 5 or 6 % of variance of the mental health criteria. To understand the place of mental health in people's lives, it is therefore important not to rely on religion as the sole variable, but to include other relevant variables like degree of physical health, socio-economic status, self-esteem, social support system and so on. If we understand mental disorders exclusively in religious terms, for example as a punishment for the nonobservation of religious laws, we might miss important alternative explanations such as those proposed for the worldwide problem of the increase in depression.

ASHIQ ALI SHAH: REPLY TO MURKEN

I wish to make some remarks about Murken's comparison of a purely naturalistic and an Islamic religion-based epistemology. I agree to some extent with the juxtaposition of the two approaches regarding their pros and cons in the inquiry of human behavior. However, I do not agree with his conclusion that the methodology adopted by both approaches should be based on theory-based hypotheses and that it should follow a hypothetico-deductive approach. In my opinion, this is the major problem with the so-called scientific approach using empirical methods. These scientific theories are reductionist fallacies of the human mind that view a human being in terms of specific proportions or percentages; they are not universal. The limitation of these theories to only certain classes of people makes their assumptions and blind application to other cultures unacceptable. For example, a handful of patients with mental disorders from Viennese bourgeois society were studied by Freud to formulate his assumptions of psychoanalysis. In the history of the so-called scientific psychology, this is an example of gross overgeneralization concerning human behavior on the basis of an unrepresentative sample. The data on behavior of rats, cats, pigeons, monkeys, and U. S. students were the basis of the theory of behaviorism obtained via logical inference. Such practices in psychology have stripped human beings of their consciousness, freedom, emotion, values, virtue, and most importantly, their soul.

Psychology is certainly not a science by any minimal scientific criterion. The psychological variables such as depression, motivation, arousal, anxiety, emotions, phobia, sociability, to name a few, are so complex that psychologists do not even agree about a precise definition of these variables, let alone their control. Unlike hard sciences, psychology could not arrange its subject matter in a homogenous hierarchical manner in which elementary facts and theories lead logically to the next ones. We have mostly a jumble of independent components of knowledge, some of which do not even recognize the authenticity of others. Denmark (1995) argued that psychology simply cannot be treated as a science in the same manner as the natural sciences.

Kuhn (1970) dismissed the claim of psychology to be a science; this on the basis of his discussion of paradigm and paradigm shift. According to Kuhn, developed sciences have paradigms whereas psychology does not. He argued that in developed sciences a paradigm shift results in a new paradigm that overthrows and replaces the old one. In psychology and other social sciences new paradigms, if we call them so, generate much enthusiasm and plenty of followers, but old ones continue to survive and sometimes flourish again after the passage of a few years. Starting from Freud's unconscious through classical and operant learning and on to the humanistic and cognitive revolution, all these approaches to explaining human behavior are flourishing and claiming to represent scientific truth despite their mutual antagonism. Once famous and absolutely dominating the stage of psychology, psychoanalysis and behaviorism claimed to explain everything through the tunnel vision of their specialization. None of the psychological theories could be refuted, or to say it in empiricists' terminology, falsified. The truth value of Murken's (this issue) assertion that "theological doctrines are not falsifiable scientific theories" could be best juxtaposed with the "pseudofalsificationism" being practiced in scientific psychology. This is due to the self-fulfilling nature of the positivistic paradigm.

In contrast, an inquiry within the Islamic framework has a different meaning and constitutes a distinct approach to the search for truth. The Islamic framework of inquiry has four levels. In descending order they are: (a) knowledge derived from Qur'an; (b) the Sunnah of the Prophet (SAW[1]), his words, deeds, and practice; (c) the *Ijma*, consensus of opinion of competent, pious Muslims; and (d) *Qiyas*, analogical deduction within the framework of Islamic law, based on human reasoning. This fourth stage of inquiry, a lower stage in the Islamic framework, is the only stage of so-called scientific inquiry.

There is another large difference in the methodology of investigation. In the Islamic approach, the prototypical researcher who acquires data and collects information is not just any academically trained individual studying college students or ordinary people, but is an intellectual and scholarly person who, nourished by the Qur'an and Sunnah, derives meanings and generates new knowledge via *Ijma* (consensus of opinion) and *Qiyas* (analogical deduction, an extension of the commandments of the Shari'ah by going from an original case to a new case and/or to new circumstances). In contrast, secularized individuals serving as prototypical researchers in the West use pure scientific empiricism. The consequences of this have included gay and lesbian marriages, older persons confined to old-age homes, premarital sex, children with unmarried parents, and crushing the weak and exploitation of others–the synonym for competition. From an Islamic point of view, this reflects unacceptable moral degradation.

The differences in the significance of religion in the West and in the Islamic world, and the unresponsive attitude of the West toward the offer of an in-depth understanding of Islam, has lead to the treatment of Islam as a religion closely comparable to Judaism and Christianity. The truth of the matter is that Islam is a way and code of life, of which religious practices are only one component (cf. Figure 2 in Khalili at al., this issue). On the contrary, in Western societies religion is regarded as a practice of specific rituals that are confined to the church and to specific moments (cf. Figure 1 in Khalili at al., this issue). Even the history of religion and scientific inquiry in the cases of Christianity and Islam are different. The scientific culture in the West emerged as a revolution against the authority of the church, a revolution that has among its martyrs the scientists who opposed the traditional teachings of the Church, women accused of witchcraft, and other victims of the infamous inquisition set up by the Church. Christianity stressed that a human being has an immortal soul yet is born in sin. There have been times when it was taught that salvation could only be achieved by blindly following the rigid uncompromising injunctions of the Church and its philosophical and scientific teachings, even when rationality and empiricism fail to support it. Hence, psychology with its various schools had to challenge these conceptions by giving their theories

---

[1]SAW [or SAAS/SAWS]; Salla Allahu 'Alaihi Wa Sallam: May the blessing and the peace of Allah be upon him; English abbr.: Pbuh.

and practices a scientific coating. That is why the majority of Western psychological theories have based themselves on a well-defined alternative, nonreligious conception about the nature of human beings.

If one wished to construct hypotheses in psychology of religion, how would one proceed on the basis of simple universal Islamic religious teachings? One would begin with these teachings: (a) Believe in one God, the only God; (b) remembrance of God is the best protection against fear and anxiety; (c) help people in distress; (d) do not drink alcohol as its harms outweigh its benefits; (e) give charity regularly to the needy; (f) do not lie; (g) do not cheat; (h) usury is the height of transgression.

These are some of the examples of religious teachings. Is there any need to construct a theory in these cases? If yes, would that theory be more complete than these universal truths? And most important overall: Is there any need for a control group? Any sensible person will not boggle his or her mind too long over the validity of these principles. The Islamic approach does not have any set of variables to inquire about the psychology of these truths. Rather, it examines the impact of following these teachings on the mental health of people. In fact, I am not against the use of a control group in principle but I am against its generalization, especially in a context where it is highly inappropriate. For example, in order to study the mediating effects (if any) of fasting or prayers, use of control groups is considered unethical and un-Islamic. There are many Muslims, however, who do not regularly pray or fast. They may serve as a control group, but they may not in fact constitute a real control group. Their not practicing the rituals might have become a habit.

The assertion that religious variables do not explain more than 5% of the total variance in any study follows from the studies in the secular framework. One may ask at this juncture about the proportion of variance explained by other contemporary psychological theories that focus only on a tiny aspect of human beings. For example, what is the contribution of learning theory in explaining the total behavioral variance when only focusing on the observable phenomena, and ignoring cognitions, feelings, emotions, physiological processes, and transcendental aspects? To be more specific, analysis shows that personality variables derived from contemporary personality theories do not account for even 5% of the total variance.

In the Islamic approach to psychology, religious and spiritual beliefs are helpful in caring for the needs of individuals. The rituals are the source of spiritual development that makes a major contribution to the psychological stability of people. Many studies in the Muslim world have indicated a tremendous role of religion in the behavior and mental health of individuals. A European psychiatrist, Schmidt (1987), reported his findings of using Islamic religious techniques in treating drug and alcohol addicts in Brunei-Darulssalam at the Third Pan Arab Congress on Psychiatry in Amman, Jordan. He tried all the methods he had learned during his training as a psychiatrist with the Muslim clients but he was unsuccessful. In the last resort he took the addicts to a camp outside the city and subjected them to a rigorous program of Islamic and physical activities involving prayers, talks, and video shows. The response of the addicts was very encouraging and they benefited much.

There are many other examples that indicate the effectiveness of Islamic beliefs and practices in managing the problem of alcoholism (Badri, 1976) and other psychological problems where other psychotherapies and psychiatric drugs failed (Badri, 1996). A number of Western psychologists and psychiatrists are becoming quite vocal about the spiritual aspects of human beings (Benson, 1996; Peck, 1990). Benson (1996) claimed that faith and belief in God are firmly embedded in human genes, that humans are literally programmed with a need for faith. It seems that he proposed a biological dimension for the Islamic concept of *Fitrah*. Ajmal (1986) argued that no systematic theory in psychology can be formulated without assuming a definite posture toward metaphysics. He believed that formulating metaphysical assumptions in psychology is especially important today, because quite a few persons are afflicted by (a) an acute dispersion into multiplicity and (b) distancing themselves from religion and God, considered as equivalent to mental disease.

As to methodology, Murken criticizes the approach of some of the papers presented at the Congress, especially those showing a relationship between religiosity and mental health. The major criticism is directed toward the correlational approach adopted in a number of empirical papers. It is argued that correlational findings might not intimate a causal relationship between religious practices and mental health because they could obscure the possible role of a third or moderator variable.

Methodologically, the coefficient of determination (r^2) assesses the extent of common variance among the variables. Also, some relationships exist among the variables that can only be examined with the help of a correlational approach and not with another method. It is naive to generalize about the weaknesses of correlational studies without considering the specific studies and the nature of their variables. The same criticism also applies to a view of scientific psychology that is too narrow. The entire disciplines of personality and of mental ability testing are founded on correlational approach since the times of Galton.

One might argue that methodological refinements could be brought about by adopting a regression approach. For example, multiple variables may be entered in a hierarchical regression to see the impact of the variables of interest on the criterion. However, the limit for the number of variables to be employed may remain controversial.

Major criticism directed at the studies seems to be relevant only in the ethnocentric–reductionist paradigm of Western psychology; but it cannot qualify as a universal syllogism, just as the claim of Western psychology, a product of laboratory experimentation with the rats and dogs, to be scientific and universal has been rejected by many psychologists (Denmark, 1995; Israel & Tajfel, 1972; Kim, 2000; Koch, 1974; Moscovici, 1972; Yang, 2000). Ajmal (1986) termed the flight of psychologists into the laboratory as an indication of their fear and the resulting wish to escape serious encounters with humans as individuals and groups, and with themselves. It may be an illusion to argue that psychological self-restriction to deal with different truths in the society is a nonreductionist scientific endeavor.

Let me end with a testimony to the scientific reliability of the Qur'an. Those researchers who are working on the scientific aspects of the Qur'an have found about 1000 verses that pertain to the scientific discoveries of our time. Just to give one example, from 1925 Edwin Hubble (1929) provided the observational evidence for the expansion of the universe. Later Stephen Hawking, author of *A Brief History of Time* (1988), explained theoretically that the universe was not static as had been previously thought but was expanding. However, this has been revealed 1400 years ago in the Qur'an: "And the firmament, We constructed with power and skill and verily We are expanding it" (Ad-Dhariyat 51: 47, The Holy Qur-An, 1410/1989). In 1512, Copernicus placed the sun motionless in the center of the solar system with all the planets revolving around it. Modern science later discovered that the sun too is in motion and not stationary. The following verse of the Qur'an indicated this: "It is He who created the night and the day, and the sun and the moon, all [the celestial bodies] swim along, each in its orbit with its own motion" (Al-Anbiya 21.33, The Holy Qur-An, 1410/1989). In other words, what was scientific for the adherents of religion of Islam 1400 years ago has now become scientific for the secular mind.

SEBASTIAN MURKEN AND ASHIQ ALI SHAH: FOLLOW-UP EXCHANGES

Sebastian Murken: Your considerations clarify the Islamic perspective, and that is an enrichment. In particular, I accept your criticism that psychology sometimes meddles with anthropology and unjustifiably claims that the resulting conceptualization of human beings is universal and the only acceptable one.

But there are a few points with which I do not quite agree. Here are my questions:

(1) On the basis of your explanations, how do you see the possibility of a joint research project? Is it possible at all to collaborate with researchers who do not share the Islamic framework? For instance, could we conduct the "same" study with Muslims in Malaysia by Islamic psychologists and in Germany by Western psychologists, and then compare the results?

(2) Accepting your methodology, how is one to research a question such as, "What is the most effective manner for teaching mathematics to a number of students of differing characteristics and backgrounds so that they all benefit most?" To my way of thinking, bringing in theories about cognition, motivation, learning,

etc. helps us to work out potentially fruitful hypotheses that can be tested in the field. Which alternative do you see in this particular case?

(3) You highlight—I believe quite well, at least historically—the benefits of Islam to mental health, science and research, etc. What about negative effects? Do they exist? Specifically, does Islam cause suffering to any person or group of persons?

(4) You blame the positivistic worldview in the West for a number of social ills. Are not societal and social issues generally too complex to be explained monocausally? And is not behaviorism largely passé except for the theory of learning, where the stick and the carrot have a long tradition? What good does it do to accuse and blame, as opposed to finding and proposing solutions? I can understand that each of us accumulates a certain amount of frustration and even anger, feels the need to eventually get rid of it, and uses upcoming opportunities to do so. Hopefully, frustration and anger thereby get out of the nervous system, and a more peaceful exchange can then take place.

Ashiq Ali Shah: I thank you for your questions, which allow me to explain some of my views in more detail. I respond to your questions one by one.

(1) I do not see any problems in that I have worked with many colleagues in the West. We are not within the Hindu system where some are untouchables. In the first place we are psychologists. We have to agree on a common strategy for any future cooperation; that is all.

Sebastian Murken: Well, I appreciate that. Maybe we can indeed set up a plan.

Ashiq Ali Shah: (2) I do not understand this question in the context of our current discussion. We are talking about religion and mental health, not mathematics. For the teaching of mathematics we have to adopt a corresponding strategy. I see this not only like the teaching of mathematics, but as much more. If the purpose of education is only to learn some specific worldly material in order to later find a job, then the methods of so-called scientific psychology are the relevant ones. On the other hand, if education is also to care for the moral and spiritual development of the child in order to prepare him or her to become a good person in this world and to be successful in the hereafter, then mere hypotheses testing may be inadequate.

(3) To answer this question I start with another question. Do you know for a fact that any divine, revealed religion harms people? I would be very interested to know about it. More specifically, I would be interested to know what you have in mind about Islam causing harm to a person or a group of people.

Sebastian Murken: You might know that I have been working as a psychotherapist for many years. I specialize in treating people with religious problems. Many of them have problems with anxiety, guilt and shame, sexuality, or their relationships partly as a result of their individual understanding of Christianity. Christianity does not prescribe harm, but still there are people who are suffering. As an example, I have discussed this in detail for the psychological processing of milleniaristic ideas (Zwingmann & Murken, 2000).

So I was wondering if there exists something similar in Islam. For example, I could imagine that certain aspects of religious teachings might cause harm to individuals, such as might occur if a woman is barred from higher education for religious reasons. As a psychologist I think that we have to look at people's actual lives and not only at religious ideals, which, I agree, are mostly very benevolent.

My suggestion is, therefore, that we understand the effects of religion and religiosity in their cultural context and the unique interaction between individuals and their own religious understanding. I hope you can agree that even people who live a very religious life might have mental problems. I have treated too many priests and clergy to believe anything else.

Ashiq Ali Shah: The answer to the point you raised is two-fold. First, it is a matter of one's worldview about religion and one's anchoring in it. Second, it is a matter of where one looks for the answer to the problem that is, the problem of causal attribution for mental problems.

First, regarding one's worldview about religion, Figures 1 and 2 (Khalili et al., this issue) describe these two worldviews. Just to mention it once again, Islam is not merely a religion, but a code of life. On the one hand, it establishes a relationship between the individual and his or her Creator and, on the other hand, it postulates one's relationship with the community and this world. The phenomenal self of human beings is hedonistic and is easily attracted toward the worldly lust. How one views religion and its practices will determine whether or not religion will lead to certain psychological problems. If one regards religion as a means to a successful life and as benevolent, then the person would not face such problems. Alternatively, if one thinks that religion is restrictive regarding some aspects of life and would like to follow one's own desires, then one might face problems. A preoccupation with individual interests in the West often conflicts with the religious teachings when individual interests are put above the collective and religious interests. Many problems are the result of this conflict between the individual and the collective interests. Islam emphasizes welfare of the individual within the social and religious context. In order to avoid these problems, one's own likings are subservient to the teachings of Islam. The message of Islam is straightforward. Allah (SWT[2]) says in the Qur'an:

O ye who believe!
Enter into Islam whole-heartedly; And follow not
The footsteps of the Satan
For he is to you An avowed enemy (Al-Baqarah, 2:208, The Holy Qur-An, 1410/1989).

---

[2]SWT; Subhanahu Wa Ta 'ala: Allah is purified of having partners or a son.

This verse of the Qur'an explains that submission is total, not partial. Many Muslims do not fulfill this criterion. As you mentioned, psychological problems arise as a result of one's understanding of Christianity. Many Muslims face the same problems because of their own understanding of Islam. If one misinterprets the Forgiveness and Mercy of God to have the liberty to commit sins and consequently encounters social and psychological problems, then it is not the religion but one's "bounded rationality" that is the perpetrator of the problems. The teachings of Islam emphasize that the human being is free and has been shown the right and the wrong through revealed guidance from time to time. Hence, each of us is responsible for his or her actions. The problems that you mentioned, that is, guilt, anxiety, shame, sexuality, and so forth, have connotations in Western psychology that are different from that in Islam. In the framework of Western psychology they pertain to the psychological problems and the aim of Western psychology is to liberate humankind from these neuroses (psychological terminology) by ridiculing religion (which refers to them as sin). In Islam, guilt, shame, and anxiety are regarded as an indicator of one's acknowledgement of wrongdoing and, therefore, are motivational in nature (i.e., motivation to reflect on and ponder over ones behavior); to ask for the Mercy and Forgiveness of God and to correct oneself. Religion has instilled the emotions of guilt, shame, and anxiety in people in order to motivate them to correct themselves—and this is for their betterment—whereas secular psychology terms them as "abnormal" in order to free the individual from every moral restriction in a sense of *liberation therapy* (Rice, 1996). These emotions lose their pathological character and become part of one's life if one follows religious teachings in letter and spirit and not according to one's own understanding and liking. These teachings are to safeguard people from such problems. The following verses of the Qur'an highlight this from different aspects.

> Nay,- whoever submits
> His whole self to Allah
> And is a doer of good,-
> He will get his reward With his Lord;
> On such shall be no fear,
> Nor shall they grieve,(Al-Baqarah, 2:112, The Holy Qur-An, 1410/1989)

> We send the Messengers
> Only to give good news
> And to warn: so those
> Who believe and mend (their lives),- upon them
> Shall be no fear, Nor shall they grieve
> (Al-An'am, 6:48, The Holy Qur-An, 1410/1989)

> Behold! Verliy on the friends/ Of Allah there is no fear,/ Nor shall they grieve;
> (Yunus, 10:62, The Holy Qur-An, 1410/1989).

The protection from psychological vows mentioned in the above verses is contingent upon the condition laid down in the aforementioned verse of Al-Baqara (2:208, The Holy Qur-An, 1410/1989).

Second, we have our own preconceived schemata to look for answers to the problems without having any clear insight, or at best having some knowledge of the subject matter and the context. I too work as a psychotherapist and have clergy as my clients. My experience shows that when their subjective values or the sociocultural circumstances conflict with the religious teachings, the problems arise as you indicated, that is, by one's individual understanding of religion—and I would like to add, "and by preoccupation with one's self by falling into a wishful circle of desires."

As to the question that you raised related to the education of females in the Muslim societies, one has to differentiate between the religious teachings, one's understanding of it, and the sociocultural context. You have mentioned that restrictions on the higher education of women in Islam (your understanding or attribution) might cause psychological problems for women. You might be surprised to know how much importance has been given to education and knowledge in Islam. There are Hadiths (sayings of the Prophet, SAW) and the verses of the Qur'an about it. In one of the Hadith, the Prophet (SAW) says "one must acquire knowledge if he or she has to travel to China" (China was regarded as the farthest country at that time). The second Hadith says, "the best ornament of a woman is education." Allah (SWT) has indicated the importance of education and knowledge many times in the Qur'an. Another Hadith says, "an illiterate cannot know even his Creator." It was Islam that opened the doors of education for everybody. There are no restrictions on women's education in Islam. Islam gave women equal rights as human beings during the dark ages when a woman was regarded as personal property. For your information, before the advent of Islam, Arabs used to bury their baby daughters in order to safeguard their pride and honor as fathers of sons. Islam termed it an act of murder and it was prohibited despite severe opposition, and gave women dignity and honor like men. There are verses in the Qur'an that highlight this. The following verse describing the day of judgment mentions:

> When the female (infant);/ Buried alive is questioned,/ For what crime She was killed;/ (At- Takwir 81:8-9, The Holy Qur-An, 1410/1989).

The confusion of Non-Muslims about Islam is due to their mixing of Islam with the social customs and tribal values. The deprivation of women from higher education or even basic education is not because of Islam but because of the local customs, tradition, and social values. There are many Muslim tribes all over the world who, in their ignorance to Islamic teachings, adhere to their customs and traditions as a matter of honor for them. These customs emphasize one's family's and the tribe's honor and pride. If honor and pride are lost, then everything is lost according to these customs. These customs, and not the Islamic teachings, are impediments in the way of women's education. Accordingly, the honor and pride of the family is lost if a woman moves in the society freely. The situation of women's education is very different among Muslim countries. Take the examples of Middle Eastern countries and some Asian and African countries where the literacy rate for women is low. In contrast, in South East Asia, for example, Malaysia and Indonesia have a high rate of literacy among women. It may be something new for you to know that the majority of the students in the Malaysian universities are women. This high ratio of women in the universities was recently a matter of concern for the education minister. It may be surprising for you to know that in the most conservative state in Malaysia, Kelantan, women virtually dominate the small and medium size businesses.

The approach to a problem affects its understanding. We will find an answer according to the way we will look at a problem with our own schemata. I think that revealed guidance provides an objective criterion for a comparative analysis.

Sebastian Murken: Thank you for this analysis of mental health and psychotherapy from an Islamic perspective. I especially agree with your (often neglected) point that psychotherapy and psychotherapists operate from a specific understanding of human nature, religion, and the world. This, of course, is value-laden and should be made transparent.

I also appreciate your distinction between Islam and culture. What I learned from our discussion is not only that my understanding of the scope of religion (Islam) is more limited than yours (cf. Figure 1 vs. Figure 2 in Khalili et al., this issue) but also my understanding of science.

I see the scope of science and the scientific process quite limited. Science will never be able to answer ultimate questions or to tell us about human nature as such. But it is an instrument to answer questions of a smaller scope.

Ashiq Ali Shah: (4) I am not blaming anybody. I am just expressing my view. This is not the first time that I have been critical of the dominance of Western psychology and its relative irrelevance to other cultures. I have been doing it since 1985. It is quite surprising that, being a product of Western education and mostly positivistic in my own research, I am that critical. I simply see both sides of the coin.

In conclusion, you are right that we should try to find solutions and not blame others. I rarely blame others for what they do, unless it is a matter that does not personally concern me. Perhaps, you got a false impression of my critique (perhaps I am wrong), as if it was directed at you. However, I have talked generally about the nature of an approach. In some cases I have to be specific or must quote in order to make my point. I would regret it if this conveyed offense.

I personally appreciate your in-depth analysis of the academic and other activities of the conference. You have taken extra pains to highlight many issues that others simply ignored or were not attentive to at all. I would appreciate having further constructive dialogue with you. This would be a good opportunity for me to learn more. I thank you for your contributions.

Sebastian Murken: Thank you for your compliments. I look forward to the publication of this important discussion and hope that it will stimulate others to join the effort of bridge building.

ACKNOWLEDGMENT

The authors thank Dr. K. Helmut Reich for his generosity of mind and his unceasing and selfless efforts to coordinate and edit this article. His constructive ideas and persuasive criticism were instrumental in bringing the article to its current form.

REFERENCES

Ajmal, M. (1986). *Muslim contributions to psychotherapy and other essays.* Islamabad: National Institute of Psychology.

Badri, M. B. (1976). *Islam and alcoholism.* Washington, DC: American Trust Publications.

Badri, M. B. (1996). Counselling and psychotherapy from an Islamic perspective. *Al-Shajarah: Journal of the International Institute of Islamic Thought & Civilisation (ISTAC, Kuala Lumpur),* 1–240.

Benson, H. (1996). *Timeless healing.* London: Simon & Schuster.

Denmark, F. L. (1995). Should we throw away the baby with the bathwater? *World Psychology, 1,* 31–36.

Feyerabend, P. (1975). *Against method.* London: New Left Books.

Feyerabend, P. (1978). *Science in a free society.* London: New Left Books.

Feyerabend, P. (1981). *Realism, rationalism and the scientific method.* Cambridge, England: Cambridge University Press.

Hanson, N. R. (1958). *Patterns of discovery: An inquiry into the conceptual foundations of science.* Cambridge, England: Cambridge University Press.

Hanson, N. R. (1971). *Observations and explanation: A guide to philosophy of science.* New York: Harper & Row.

Hawking, S. (1988). *A brief history of time: From the big bang to black holes.* London: Bantam.

Hood, R. W., Jr., Ghorbani, N., Watson, P. J., Ghramaleki, A. F., Bing, M. N., Davison, H. K., Morris, R. J., & Williamson, W. P. (2001). Dimensions of the mysticism scale: Confirmation of the three-factor structure in the United States and Iran. *Journal for the Scientific Study of Religion, 40*(4), 691–705.

Hubble, E. (1929). *A relation between distance and radial velocity among extra-galactic nebulae.* Proceedings of the National Academy of Sciences, (Vol. 15; 3, March 15). Retrieved June 26, 2002 from http://antwrp.gsfc.nasa.gov/diamond_jubilee/1996/hub?1929.html

Israel, J., & Tajfel, H. (1972). *The context of social psychology: A critical assessment.* London: Academic.

Kim, U. (2000). Indigenous, cultural, and cross-cultural psychology. A theoretical, conceptual, and epistemological analysis. *Asian Journal of Social Psychology, 3,* 265-287.

Kitchener, R. F. (Ed.). (1988). *The world view of contemporary physics. Does it need a new metaphysics?* Albany: State University of New York Press.

Koch, S. (1974). Psychology as a science. In S. C. Brown (Ed.), *Philosophy of psychology.* London: Macmillan.

Kuhn, T. S. (1970). *The structure of scientific revolution.* Chicago: The University of Chicago Press.

Lakatos, I. (1970). Falsification and the methodology of scientific research programmes. In I. Lakatos & A. Musgrave (Eds.), *Criticism and the growth of knowledge* (pp. 91–196). Cambridge, England: Cambridge University Press.

Lakatos, I. (1978). *The methodology of scientific research programmes.* Cambridge, England: Cambridge University Press.

Lakoff, G. & Johnson, M. (1999). *Philosophy in the flesh. The embodied mind and its challenge to Western thought.* New York: Basic Books.

Laudan, L. (1990). *Science and relativism. Some key controversies in the philosophy of science.* Chicago: University of Chicago Press.

Luhmann, N. (1995). *Social systems* (J. Bednarz, Jr., Trans., with D. Baecker). Stanford, CA: Stanford University Press.

Moscovici, S. (1972). Society and theory in social psychology. In J. Israel & H. Tajfel (Eds.), *The context of social psychology: A critical assessment.* London: Academic.

Peck, M. S. (1990). *The road less traveled.* London: Arrow Books.

Popper, K. R. (1935). *Die Logik der Forschung* [The logic of scientific discovery]. Vienna, Austria: Springer.

Popper, K. R. (1963). *Conjectures and refutations.* London: Routledge & Kegan Paul.

Popper, K. R. (1972). *Objective knowledge.* Oxford, England: Oxford University Press.

Reich, K. H. (2002). *Developing the horizons of the mind: Relational and contextual reasoning and the resolution of cognitive conflicts.* Cambridge, England; Cambridge University Press.

Rice, J. S. (1996). *A disease of one's own: Psychotherapy, addiction, and the emergence of co- dependency.* New Brunswick, NJ: Transaction.

Schmidt, K. (1987, April). Paper presented at the Third Pan Arab Congress on Psychiatry in Amman, Jordan.

The Holy Qur-An. (1410/1989). *English translation of the meanings and commentary. The Presidency of Islamic Researchers, IFTA, Call and guidance.* Mushaf Al-Madinah An-Nabawiyah: King Fahd Holy Qur-an Printing Complex.

Yang, K. S. (2000). Monocultural and cross-cultural indigenous approaches: The royal road to the development of a balanced global psychology. *Asian Journal of Social Psychology, 3,* 241–264.

Zwingmann, C., & Murken, S. (2000). Coping with an uncertain future: religiosity and millenarianism. *Archiv für Religionspsychologie, 23,* 11–28.

THE INTERNATIONAL JOURNAL FOR THE PSYCHOLOGY OF RELIGION, 12(4), 255–276

RESEARCH

Negatively Reinforcing Personal Extrinsic Motivations: Religious Orientation, Inner Awareness, and Mental Health in Iran and the United States

P. J. Watson
Department of Psychology
University of Tennessee at Chattanooga

Nima Ghorbani
Department of Psychology
University of Tehran

H. Kristl Davison
Department of Psychology
University of Hartford

Mark N. Bing
Department of Psychology
University of Tennessee at Chattanooga

Ralph W. Hood, Jr.
Department of Psychology
University of Tennessee at Chattanooga

Ahad Framarz Ghramaleki
Department of Islamic Philosophy
University of Tehran

Requests for reprints should be sent to P. J. Watson, Psychology/Department #2803, 350 Holt Hall–615 McCallie, University of Tennessee at Chattanooga, Chattanooga, TN 37403. E-mail: paul-watson@utc.edu

In Iranian and American samples, a new Negatively Reinforcing Personal Extrinsic Religious Motivations Scale contained four factors. These four Personal-Negative factors correlated positively with the Allport and Ross Intrinsic and Extrinsic Religious Orientation Scales. In correlations with measures of an inner psychological awareness, Intrinsic and Extrinsic constructs predicted greater Self-Consciousness and Self-Knowledge in Iran, but not in the United States. In both cultures, however, intrinsicness was associated with lower Alexithymia and greater Emotional Intelligence whereas the opposite was true of extrinsicness, especially after partialing out the Intrinsic Scale. A few findings suggested that Extrinsic motivations might have positive mental health implications, but linkages with Anxiety, Depression, Perceived Stress, and Self-Esteem overwhelmingly depicted intrinsicness as adjusted and extrinsicness as maladjusted. Each Personal-Negative factor displayed evidence of incremental validity. Factor analysis of all religious orientation variables in each sample yielded two components, a general religious motivation factor and a bipolar Intrinsic dimension. Iranians were higher on several Extrinsic measures. Americans displayed higher Intrinsic scores. These data suggested that religious motivation was more highly integrated within the Iranians and that Allportian concepts supplied a productive conceptual framework for understanding Iranian Muslim as well as American Christian religious commitments.

Progress in a truly international psychology of religion presumably will parallel progress in other areas of cross-cultural psychological research. McCrae (2001) recently described the challenges in terms of a need for three levels of analysis. Relative to the psychology of religion, *transcultural* concerns would involve the search for universals in religious psychological functioning in contrast to the culturally specific focus of *intracultural* studies. *Intercultural* investigations would explore differences between religious traditions. McCrea applied these categories to an extensive cross-cultural literature on personality traits. Specifically, he reexamined data from over 23,000 subjects representing 26 different cultures in an intercultural "pilot study" of the Big-Five personality traits. Cross-cultural work in the psychology of religion is obviously at a much more preliminary stage of development. Even tentative generalizations about the three levels of analysis require many more studies that simultaneously examine believers from different traditions and that sample more than the typically employed English-speaking, primarily Christian subjects (Hood, Spilka, Hunsberger, & Gorsuch, 1996, p. 448).

The promise of such research was illustrated in a recent extension of Allport's (1950) interpretation of religious motivation to Iranian Muslims along with American Christians (Ghorbani, Watson, Ghramaleki, Morris, & Hood, 2002). Allport distinguished between non-instrumental and instrumental reasons for being religious and developed Intrinsic and Extrinsic Religious Orientation Scales to measure the difference (Allport & Ross, 1967). Within a non-instrumental, Intrinsic motivation, religion theoretically serves as a master motive with the believer sincerely trying to live his or her faith. Within an instrumental, Extrinsic orientation, religion instead serves as a means to sometimes-selfish ends. Allport hypothesized—and research usually, though not invariably—has confirmed that the Intrinsic and Extrinsic Scales predict adjustment and maladjustment, respectively (Donahue, 1985). Iranian Muslims in fact displayed that basic pattern.

Kirkpatrick (1989) used factor analysis to document the multidimensional complexity of the Extrinsic Scale. An Extrinsic–Personal (E–P) factor reflected the use of religion to accomplish positive personal outcomes (e.g., "the primary purpose of prayer is to gain relief and protection"). An Extrinsic–Social (E–S) factor described the use of religion as a means for achieving social benefits (e.g., "one reason for my being a church member is that such membership helps establish a person in the community"). A remaining group of Extrinsic–Residual (E–R) items expressed a form of commitment that was antithetical to intrinsicness (e.g., "although I am a religious person, I refuse to let religious considerations influence my everyday affairs"). In the Iranian and American samples, these Extrinsic measures displayed similar though not identical relationships with other religious variables. With the Iranians, they also predicted maladjustment.

Recent speculation has suggested that Allport was overly pessimistic in his evaluation of extrinsicness (Pargament, 1992). The previous Iranian–American study analyzed that possibility by attempting to accomplish a more comprehensive assessment of the Extrinsic motivation. New Extrinsic Scales first assumed that religious motivations could be directed toward accomplishing "this-worldly" goals or toward reaching heaven in the next. They also might point toward positively reinforcing consequences by describing efforts to achieve a perceived "good" or toward negatively reinforcing outcomes by defining attempts to avoid or escape from a perceived "bad." With regard to this-worldly concerns, goals might focus on personal psychological functioning, the social circumstances of an individual, or cultural well-being. Use of these new measures yielded only slight support for the hypothesis that positively rather than negatively reinforcing motivations would predict adjustment. The data instead revealed that all aspects of extrinsicness were associated with undesirable mental health implications.

PRESENT STUDY

In the present project, additional Iranian and American samples were examined in order to clarify the Negatively Reinforcing Personal Extrinsic Motivations Scale developed in the earlier investigation. This 23-item Personal–Negative Scale was an especially clear predictor of unhealthy psychological functioning. It also displayed linkages with maladjustment in the second step of multiple regressions after the Intrinsic, E–P, E–S, and E–R measures had been entered in on the first step. This instrument, in other words, displayed incremental validity. In this study, Personal–Negative items were factor analyzed, and the obtained components then were utilized to accomplish three basic objectives. First, the religious motivational implications of these factors were ascertained in correlations with the Allport and Ross Scales and in multiple regressions that examined their incremental validity.

Second, the Personal–Negative and other religious orientation measures were used to test Browning's (1987) assertion that religions supply "concepts and technologies for the ordering of the inner life" (p. 2). This idea seemed consistent with Muslim and Christian claims that knowledge of God is intimately connected with knowledge of the self. Early Muslim leaders, for instance, argued that "someone who knows oneself, knows God" (Frozanfar, 1370/1991, p. 167) and that "self-knowledge is the most useful form of knowledge" and a sign of wisdom (Khansari, 1366/1987, p. 25, p. 297). Within Christian traditions, Calvin (1559/1960) argued that "without knowledge of self there is no knowledge of God" and that "without knowledge of God there is no knowledge of self" (pp. 35–37). Religious orientation variables, therefore, were correlated with constructs that presumably would reflect an "ordering of the inner life" of the self. These included measures of Self-Consciousness, Self-Knowledge, Alexithymia, and Emotional Intelligence.

The Self-Consciousness Scales of Fenigstein, Scheier, and Buss (1975) include Private Self-Consciouness, Public Self-Consciousnesss, and Social Anxiety subscales. Private Self-Consciousness monitors an introspective openness to inner thoughts and feelings and contains two factors (Mittal & Balasubramanian, 1987). The Self-Reflectiveness factor is evident in such self-reports as, "I'm always trying to figure myself out." Internal State Awareness is illustrated in the claim that "I'm generally attentive to my inner feelings." Public Self-Consciousness records attentiveness to how the self appears to others and also includes two factors: Appearance Consciousness (e.g., "I'm usually aware of my appearance") and Style Consciousness (e.g., "I'm concerned about what other people think about me"). Social Anxiety measures emotional discomfort in the presence of others (e.g., "I have trouble working when someone is watching me"). In previous research, the Public Self-Consciousness factors have displayed positive, negative, and nonsignificant relationships with a broad array of mental health variables. Internal State Awareness, in contrast, usually predicted adjustment whereas Self-Reflectiveness and Social Anxiety were indicative of maladjustment (e.g., Watson, Hickman, Morris, Stutz, & Whiting, 1994; Watson, Morris, & Hood, 1988a; Watson, Morris, Ramsey, Hickman, & Waddell, 1996).

Reflective and Experiential Self-Knowledge Scales were created in this and a series of associated studies in order to operationalize an adaptive form of knowing the self (Ghorbani, Watson, Bing, Davison, & LeBreton, 2002). Reflective Self-Knowledge represents an active cognitive processing of information about the self in terms of its past and involves efforts to develop progressively more sophisticated schemas of self-understanding. This form of Self- Knowledge is illustrated in the self-report, "Through reflection, I am able to see how both my positive and negative moods influence how I communicate with others." Experiential Self-Knowledge theoretically represents a dynamic openness to experiences of the self in the present. This openness provides the principal data of personal experience that the self presumably needs to meet the challenges that confront it and to achieve the goals that motivate it. One item states, for instance, "I am immediately aware of the ongoing changes in my feelings."

Alexithymia literally means "without words for emotions," and the 20-item Toronto Alexithymia Scale (Bagby, Parker, & Taylor, 1994) includes three components of this maladjusted lack of an "inner awareness" (Bagby, Taylor, & Parker, 1994; Parker, Taylor, & Bagby, 2001). The Externally Oriented Thinking factor is exemplified in the statement that "I prefer to just let things happen rather than to understand why they turned out that way." Difficulty Identifying Feelings is obvious in such self-reports as, "When I am upset, I don't know if I am sad, frightened, or angry." Difficulty Describing Feelings appears in the assertion, "It is difficult for me to find the right words for my feelings."

Trait Meta-Mood Scales operationalize an input–process–output information-processing model of a psychologically healthy Emotional Intelligence (Salovey, Mayer, Goldman, Turvey, & Palfai, 1995). The Attention Scale records the psychological input of emotional information (e.g., "I pay a lot of attention to how I feel"). A Clarity Scale expresses an active processing of those inputs (e.g., "I almost always know exactly how I am feeling"). The Repair Scale describes efforts to respond adaptively to emotional information that has been processed (e.g., "I try to think good thoughts no matter how badly I feel").

Third and finally, the adjustment implications of all religious orientation variables were examined by administering measures of Self-Esteem (Rosenberg, 1965), Perceived Stress (Cohen, Kamarck, & Mermelstein, 1983) and Anxiety and Depression (Costello & Comrey, 1967). The Rosenberg instrument is an often-used index of healthy global self-esteem (e.g., "on the whole, I am satisfied with myself"). As a correlate of disturbed psychological functioning (e.g., Chang, 1998), the Perceived Stress Scale presents a series of questions that ask how frequently a person experiences stressful life events (e.g., "in the last month, how often have you felt difficulties were piling up so high that you could not overcome them?"). Costello and Comrey Scales monitor dispositional depression (e.g., "I wish I were never born") and anxiety (e.g., "I am a very nervous person").

HYPOTHESES

In summary, factors from the 23-item Personal–Negative Scale were identified and then correlated with religious orientation, inner awareness, and mental health. Relative to an Allportian perspective, the hypothesis was that the Intrinsic Scale would correlate directly with adjustment (Self-Esteem, Self-Knowledge, Emotional Intelligence, and Internal State Awareness) and inversely with maladjustment (Anxiety, Depression, Perceived Stress, Alexithymia, Self-Reflectiveness, and Social Anxiety). Expectations for the Extrinsic measures were opposite. Appearance and Style Consciousness have displayed no consistent mental health implications, but as operationalizations of inner awareness, the hypothesis was that they would predict greater religious motivation generally. The prior Iranian–American study documented that unambiguous understandings of religious orientation sometimes required the use of partial correlations (Ghorbani, Watson, Ghramaleki, Morris, & Hood, 2002). Especially in Iran, some Extrinsic associations with unhealthy self-functioning appeared only after partialing out the Intrinsic Scale. Hence, positive Extrinsic correlations with adjustment, for instance, might support recent, more sanguine descriptions of extrinsicness (Pargament, 1992), or they might merely reflect the beneficial influences of intrinsicness that Allport originally emphasized. In such cases, interpretative clarity obviously would require partial correlations controlling for the Intrinsic Scale.

METHOD

Participants

Research participants were university student volunteers from Iran and the United States. The Iranian sample was from Tehran and included 116 females, 111 males, and 4 individuals who failed to indicate gender. Their average age was 21.97 (SD = 2.91). Of the Americans, 86 were females with 134 males. The average age of this sample was 20.30 (SD = 3.81). All Iranians were Persian Muslims. The Americans attended a branch campus of a large southeastern state university system and displayed greater racial and religious diversity. These students were 68.2% Caucasian, 25.0% African–American, and 6.8% various other racial groups. Religious commitments were 41.4% Baptist, 11.8% Methodist, 9.5% Catholic, 9.5% Presbyterian, 5.0% Church of Christ, 2.3% Church of God, 7.3% "Other Protestant," and 13.2% simply "other."

Measures

Two questionnaire booklets were created by the researchers to include scales for use in several related investigations. Booklets were constructed to be as similar as possible across both samples. Through extensive e-mail conversations, the first two authors discussed meanings and nuances of English terms before settling upon appropriate Persian translations for all instruments. The accuracy of those translations was confirmed by having someone unfamiliar with the project translate the Persian statements back into English.

Except for the Perceived Stress, Self-Knowledge, and Religious Orientation Scales, participants responded to all questionnaire items along a 5-point Likert scale ranging from 0 (*strongly agree*) to 4 (*strongly disagree*). Options for Perceived Stress varied along a 0 (*never*) to 4 (*very often*) response format. For Self-Knowledge, possible responses were 0 (*largely untrue*), 1 (*somewhat untrue*), 2 (*neither true nor untrue*), 3 (*somewhat true*), and 4 (*largely true*). Personal-Negative statements were associated with a 4-point Likert scale: 0 (*I definitely disagree*), 1 (*I tend to disagree*), 2 (*I tend to agree*), and 3 (*I definitely agree*). Allport and Ross Scales were administered according to standard instructions (Robinson & Shaver, 1973).

Prior to other data analyses, internal reliabilities were computed for all scales in each sample separately. Any item that failed to display a positive item–to–total correlation in either sample was eliminated from both. This procedure in the present and previous Iranian–American studies improved internal reliabilities, produced more robust and consistent correlations, and yielded data that conformed with theoretical expectations. Based on this criterion, single statements were dropped from the Attention, Externally Oriented Thinking, and Perceived Stress measures. Except for the Self-Consciousness and Self-Knowledge variables, details about all psychological measures were reported in a previous cross-cultural analysis of emotional information processing (Ghorbani, Bing, Watson, Davison, & Mack, in press), including the number of items associated with each construct, the specific statements that were eliminated, culture-specific alphas, descriptive statistics, and correlations among all nonreligious measures. This manuscript is available from the authors upon request.

With regard to measures not explored in this earlier investigation, two statements dealing with religious behaviors were removed from the Intrinsic Scale because they exhibited slightly negative item–to–total correlations in the Iranians. One stated, "If I were to join a church/religious group, I would prefer to join (1) a Bible/Qur'an study group or (2) a social fellowship," with tendencies to favor the first choice reflecting an Intrinsic motivation. The other said, "If not prevented by unavoidable circumstances, I attend church/the mosque" from "more than once a week" to "less than once a month."

For theoretical reasons, the earlier cross-cultural analysis of emotion information processing examined only the Private and Public Self-Consciousness subscales, not Social Anxiety nor the four more specific Self-Consciousness factors. Acceptable coefficient alphas were observed for the 4-item Social Anxiety subscale (Iran, $\alpha = .77$, M response per item $= 2.16$, $SD = 1.01$; United States, $\alpha = .64$, $M = 2.13$, $SD = 0.88$). Slightly lower reliabilities were obtained for the 4-item Internal State Awareness factor (Iran, $\alpha = .61$, $M = 2.65$, $SD = 0.75$; United States, $\alpha = .56$, $M = 2.96$, $SD = 0.60$) and for the 4-item Self-Reflectiveness measure (Iran,

$\alpha = .67$, $M = 2.46$, $SD = 0.83$; United States, $\alpha = .60$, $M = 2.15$, $SD = 0.77$). Similar values were obvious for the 3-item Appearance Consciousness (Iran, $\alpha = .69$, $M = 2.76$, $SD = 0.95$; United States, $\alpha = .51$, $M = 2.73$, $SD = 0.81$) and for the 4-item Style Consciousness (Iran, $\alpha = .66$, $M = 2.66$, $SD = 0.83$; United States, $\alpha = .64$, $M = 2.13$, $SD = 0.88$) factors. For the two 13-item Self-Knowledge Scales, acceptable internal consistencies were evident for both Reflective (Iran, $\alpha = .86$, $M = 2.45$, $SD = 0.71$; United States, $\alpha = .81$, $M = 2.76$, $SD = 0.55$) and Experiential (Iran, $\alpha = .90$, $M = 2.45$, $SD = 0.72$; United States, $\alpha = .86$, $M = 2.74$, $SD = 0.56$) Self-Knowledge.

Procedure

Scales were administered to both samples in the same order and with the same basic instructions. The first booklet contained all but the Self-Knowledge measures of inner awareness and mental health. The second booklet began with statements used to create the new Self-Knowledge Scales. Religious orientation measures came next with Personal–Negative items interspersed among those from the Allport and Ross Scales. Participants responded to these questionnaire booklets in groups of approximately 50 or less. Completion of all measures was accomplished within an hour and a half in virtually every instance.

Americans marked their reactions to all questionnaire items on standardized answer sheets that subsequently were read by optical scanning equipment into a computer data file. Iranians noted their responses on paper answer sheets, and these data were entered into the computer manually. To insure accuracy, the Iranian data were double-checked after they had been entered into the data file.

After internal reliabilities of all instruments were maximized, items from the Personal–Negative Scale were factor analyzed. Components then were constructed and correlated with all other variables in each sample separately. Partial correlations helped clarify some of these data. Multiple regressions examined the incremental validity of the Personal–Negative factors, and a description of all religious orientation variables in each sample was accomplished in a summarizing factor analysis. Finally, a MANOVA followed by ANOVAs where appropriate were used to assess all religious orientation variables in terms of Culture, Gender, and Culture × Gender interaction effects.

RESULTS

In this investigation, data analysis focused on the religious orientation measures. Relationships among the inner awareness and mental health variables were described in the previously mentioned study (Ghorbani, Bing, Watson, Davison, & Mack, in press). Four generalizations about those data supplied the necessary interpretative background for this project. First, no major contrasts appeared in the cross-cultural implications of any measure. A clear index of psychological health in America, for example, never predicted psychological dysfunction in Iran, or vice versa. Second, correlations matched expectations for operationalizations of adjustment (e.g., Self-Esteem and Emotional Intelligence) and maladjustment (Depression, Anxiety, Perceived Stress, Alexithymia, and Social Anxiety). Third, Private and Public Self- Consciousness factors displayed no conceptually noteworthy deviations from previously published findings (e.g., Watson et al., 1988a; Watson et al., 1994; Watson et al., 1996). Finally, the new Reflective and Experiential Self-Knowledge instruments in fact recorded healthier psychological functioning.

Several strategies were pursued in factor analyzing the Personal–Negative items. Culture-specific analyses defined roughly similar factor structures across both samples, but with cross-cultural variations in the loadings of some statements on different factors. With the two samples combined, the same general factors appeared, and item loadings described clear and meaningful components. The combined data, therefore, were employed. A principal components analysis with a varimax rotation yielded the four factors presented in Table 1. The *Religion Dependent Self* factor contained 10 statements describing the use of religion to avoid negative feelings of depression, anxiety, guilt, and inadequacy. The four *Insecurity* items articulated the perhaps effortful attempts of an individual to use religion to cope with insecurity, meaninglessness, and guilt. The Prayer and Practice factor contained four statements that most importantly reflected the use of prayer for negatively reinforcing psychological purposes. Five statements expressing a motivation to avoid the anger and punishment of God formed a final *Fear of God* factor.

Correlations among and means, standard deviations, and coefficient alphas for all religious variables are presented in Table 2. All or almost all but the E–R religious orientation measures co-varied directly in both cultures. In the United States, E–R items predicted lower intrinsicness while also displaying positive associations with E–S and with 3 out of the 4 Personal–Negative factors. In Iran, these residual items correlated positively with E–S and negatively with the Intrinsic and E–P constructs. Most internal reliabilities were acceptable for research purposes (> .60), but lower coefficient alphas for some of these religious (e.g., for E–S and E–R in Iran) and also for some of the inner awareness variables (e.g., Internal State Awareness and Appearance Consciousness) revealed a need for caution in interpreting these data.

Striking cultural contrasts appeared in linkages of religious orientation with the Self- Consciousness and Self-Knowledge Scales (see Table 3). In the Iranians, all but the E–S and E–R religious variables displayed consistent direct associations with all of these constructs. In contrast, absolutely no relationships appeared between these two sets of variables in the Americans. E–R items correlated positively with Social Anxiety in Iran and negatively with Reflective Self-Knowledge in America. No significant relationship with any measure of self- functioning appeared for the E–S factor.

TABLE 1
Factors From Extrinsic Personal Negative Scale

Factor 1: Religion Dependent Self (Eigenvalue = 8.91; Percent Variance = 38.75%)
1. If I did not believe in God, I would have no reason for getting out of bed in the morning. (.70)
2. Religion is my only hope for overcoming the imperfections in my personality. (.69)
3. If I do not follow the commands of my religion, I see myself as a bad person. (.65)
4. I always try to think about God so that I can avoid unhappiness. (61)
5. I try not to neglect my religious duties, because if I do, I feel tense. (.61)
6. If I were not religious, I would be depressed all the time. (.60)
7. Without the demands of my religion, I would be unable to control my emotions. (.56)
8. I believe that personal misery results when we behave in ways that our religion identifies as evil. (.50).
9. If I did not do all that my religion required of me, I would be a bad person in my own eyes. (.49)
10. An awareness of my own personal inadequacies is a main reason why I need God. (.44)

Factor 2: Insecurity (Eigenvalue = 1.56; Percent Variance = 6.79%)
1. I try to believe in God because I am constantly tortured by the seeming meaninglessness of life. (.75)
2. An attempt to overcome my sense of insecurity is a main reason for my being religious. (.73)
3. A sense of insecurity is my main reason for having a religious life. (.65)
4. I try to follow the morality of my religion because I know that God will make me feel guilty if I do not. (.62)

Factor 3: Prayer and Practice (Eigenvalue = 1.37; Percent Variance = 5.95%)
1. I pray in order to eliminate my feelings of misery. (.82)
2. I pray mainly to eliminate my unhappiness. (.70)
3. I pray because I do not want to experience the anxiety and worry that I feel when I do not pray. (.64)
4. I follow the commands of my faith because I do not want to feel like a failure. (.57)

Factor 4: Fear of God (Eigenvalue = 1.14; Percent Variance = 4.94%)
1. My fear of God's authority is the primary motivation behind my attempt to follow the commands of my religion. (.71)
2. My fear of angering God is the primary motivation behind my attempt to avoid sin. (.66)
3. I am religious because I know God sometimes punishes people when they fail to be as religious as they should. (.60)
4. We should remain faithful so that God does not punish us. (.52)
5. If I behave immorally, I am sure that God will punish me and make me miserable. (.45)

Note. Factor loadings are indicated in the parentheses.

To what extent did the adjustment of intrinsicness mediate linkages of extrinsicness with the Self-Consciousness and Self-Knowledge variables? Again, this question was answered in partial correlations that controlled for the Intrinsic Scale. In the Iranians, many, but not all, of the significant zero-order relationships were explained by Intrinsic variance. Findings for Social Anxiety were largely unaffected, but Personal–Negative factors no longer displayed reliable associations with Internal State Awareness or with Reflective and Experiential Self-Knowledge. Only Fear of God remained tied to Self-Reflectiveness ($.14, p < .05$). The Religious Dependent Self factor no longer predicted Appearance Consciousness, and other Personal–Negative relationships with Public Self-Consciousness were reduced, ranging from .15 ($p < .05$) between Insecurity and Appearance Consciousness to .22 ($p < .05$) between Fear of God and Style Consciousness. The E–P linkage with Internal State Awareness was eliminated. Other E–P associations were diminished and varied from .28 ($p < .05$) with Self-Reflectiveness to .38 ($p < .05$) with Style Consciousness. Negative relationships appeared for E–S with Reflective (–.17, $p < .07$) and Experiential (–.13, $p < .05$) Self-Knowledge, and positive correlations of .14 ($ps < .05$) emerged for E–R with both Appearance and Style Consciousness. In the American sample, partial correlations produced only two effects. The Religious Dependent Self factor correlated positively with Appearance Consciousness (.15, $p < .05$), and Fear of God correlated negatively with Reflective Self-Knowledge (–.16, $p < .05$).

Iranian religious orientation relationships with Alexithymia, Emotional Intelligence, and mental health are summarized in Table 4. The Intrinsic Scale and, to a lesser extent, the E–P factor predicted adjustment, whereas the E–R items correlated with maladjustment. Other Extrinsic measures displayed positive connections with the Difficulty Identifying and/or the Difficulty Describing Feelings factors of Alexithymia. Prayer and Practice was associated with slightly higher levels of Anxiety. However, the Prayer and Practice and Religious Dependent Self

TABLE 2
Correlations Among and Descriptive Statistics for Religious Variables[a]

Variables	1.	2.	3.	4.	5.	6.	7.	8.
Personal Negative Factors								
1. Religious Dependent Self	—	.66***	.69***	.74***	.70***	.66***	.47***	–.01
2. Insecurity	.44***	—	.63***	.72***	.43***	.59***	.35***	.05
3. Prayer and Practice	.53***	.48***	—	.69***	.48***	.69***	.50***	.08
4. Fear of God	.61***	.47***	.51***	—	.50***	.64***	.41***	.10
Allport and Ross Measures								
5. Intrinsic	.63***	.05	.22**	.33***	—	.64***	.31***	–.24***
6. Extrinsic–Personal	.43***	.34***	.64***	.41***	.30***	—	.28***	–.15*
7. Extrinsic–Social	.21**	.51***	.45***	.27***	.02	.37***	—	.15*
8. Extrinsic–Residuals	–.13	.49***	.20**	.16*	–.48***	.12	.42***	—
Descriptive Statistics								
Iran								
Mean[b]	1.63	1.59	1.37	1.60	2.04	1.81	1.07	1.09
Standard Deviation	.68	.71	.83	.72	.63	.82	.72	.59
Coefficient Alpha	.86	.68	.80	.77	.71	.67	.59	.53
The United States								
Mean	1.43	.94	1.34	1.36	2.27	1.77	.89	1.11
Standard Deviation	.65	.68	.77	.76	.66	.73	.70	.65
Coefficient Alpha	.88	.77	.79	.83	.81	.66	.66	.68

[a]Correlations for the Iranian sample are above the diagonal, whereas those for the Americans are below. [b]Means represent the average response per item for each measure.
*$p < .05$. **$p < .01$. ***$p < .001$.

TABLE 3

Correlations of Personal Negative Factors and Religious Orientation Measures With Self-Consciousness and Self-Knowledge in the Iranian and American Samples

Psychological Measures	Religious Measures							
	RDS	INS	PP	FG	INT	E–P	E–S	E–R
Iranian Sample								
Internal State Awareness	.26***	.10	.19**	.18**	.39***	.35***	.04	−.05
Self–Reflectiveness	.34***	.26***	.26***	.31***	.40***	.45***	.04	−.06
Appearance Consciousness	.29***	.27***	.33***	.32***	.32**	.44***	.12	.05
Style Consciousness	.34***	.27***	.34***	.35***	.33***	.48***	.09	.05
Social Anxiety	.23***	.21**	.21**	.19**	.13*	.23***	.10	.15*
Reflective Self–Knowledge	.32***	.28***	.22**	.27***	.45***	.52***	.00	−.12
Experiential Self–Knowledge	.27***	.19**	.19**	.19**	.42***	.47***	.02	−.12
American Sample								
Internal State Awareness	.06	−.06	−.10	−.02	.06	.00	−.08	−.07
Self–Reflectiveness	−.01	.11	.06	−.08	−.07	−.08	.04	−.07
Appearance Consciousness	.10	.05	.07	.07	−.04	.11	.10	.03
Style Consciousness	.02	.06	.06	−.04	−.01	.03	.06	−.06
Social Anxiety	−.07	.02	.00	−.05	−.12	.03	−.02	.05
Reflective Self–Knowledge	−.01	−.06	.00	−.11	.12	−.06	−.06	−.14*
Experiential Self–Knowledge	.06	−.08	−.08	.04	.12	.02	−.05	−.08

Note. Personal Negative Factors are Religious Dependent Self (RDS), Insecurity (INS), Prayer and Practice (PP), and Fear of God (FG). Religious Orientation measures are the Intrinsic Scale (INT), the Extrinsic–Personal (E–P) and Extrinsic–Social (E–S) factors, and the Extrinsic–Residual (E–R) items.
*$p < .05$. **$p < .01$. ***$p < .001$.

TABLE 4

Correlations of Personal Negative Factors and Religious Orientation Measures With Alexithymia, Emotional Intelligence, and Mental Health in the Iranian Sample

Psychological Measures	Religious Measures							
	RDS	INS	PP	FG	INT	E–P	E–S	E–R
Alexithymia								
Difficulty Identifying Feelings	.18**	.24***	.24***	.24***	−.05	.10	.18**	.25***
Difficulty Describing Feelings	.14*	.15*	.11	.10	.04	.09	−.03	.00
Externally Oriented Thinking	−.17*	−.03	−.04	−.05	−.31***	−.20**	.03	.11
Emotional Intelligence								
Attention	.04	.04	.00	.11	.13*	.15*	−.12	.00
Clarity	.06	−.03	−.03	−.01	.23***	.12	−.05	−.25***
Repair	.21**	.08	.14*	.20**	.37***	.36***	.03	−.14*
Mental Health								
Anxiety	.11	.12	.14*	.09	−.07	.08	.05	.17*
Depression	−.07	.03	−.01	−.01	−.30***	−.14*	.04	.20**
Perceived Stress	−.04	.07	.06	.05	−.22**	−.05	.03	.12
Self–Esteem	.12	.00	.09	.04	.35***	.21**	−.01	−.22**

Note. Personal Negative Factors are Religion Dependent Self (RDS), Insecurity (INS), Prayer and Practice (PP), and Fear of God (FG). Religious Orientation measures are the Intrinsic Scale (INT), the Extrinsic–Personal (E–P) and Extrinsic–Social (E–S) factors, and the Extrinsic–Residual (E–R) items.
*$p < .05$. **$p < .01$. ***$p < .001$.

factors correlated positively with Repair, and the Religion Dependent Self also displayed an inverse connection with Externally Oriented Thinking.

Once again, partial correlations documented the important influence of Intrinsic variance on these Extrinsic relationships. The Religious Dependent Self partial correlation with Externally Oriented Thinking was positive rather than negative (.14, $p < .05$). The direct association of this factor with Repair also was removed, and new linkages appeared with Clarity (–.15), Anxiety (.23), Depression (.21), Perceived Stress (.18), and Self-Esteem (–.19, $ps < .05$). Additional evidence of Insecurity relationships with maladjustment appeared in partial correlations with Externally Oriented Thinking (.18), Clarity (–.16), Anxiety (.18), Depression (.20), Perceived Stress (.23), and Self-Esteem (–.19, $ps < .05$). Similar effects were observed for Prayer and Practice with Externally Oriented Thinking (.21), Clarity (–.19), Depression (.19), and Perceived Stress (.24, $ps < .05$). The positive zero-order Prayer and Practice correlation with Repair also disappeared. Fear of God exhibited partial correlations with Externally Oriented Thinking (.21), Clarity (–.16), Anxiety (.16), Depression (.19), Perceived Stress (.22), and Self-Esteem (–.19, $ps < .05$). The previously observed positive linkage between Fear of God and Repair was eliminated.

In these partial correlations, E–P no longer displayed significant inverse relationships with Externally Oriented Thinking and Depression, nor positive correlations with Attention and Self- Esteem. The reliable E–P connection with Repair was reduced, but not eliminated (.16, $p < .05$), but new associations appeared with Difficulty Identifying Feelings (.18), Anxiety (.18), and Perceived Stress (.14, $ps < .05$). For E–S, significant partial correlations appeared with Externally Oriented Thinking (.19), Attention (–.17), Depression (.14), and Self-Esteem (–.14, $ps < .05$). E–R data remained largely unaffected, except that the inverse tie with Repair became nonsignificant.

Table 5 reviews the same zero-order relationships for the American sample. The Intrinsic Scale and E–R items once again predicted adjustment and maladjustment, respectively. The Religious Dependent Self factor displayed a slight positive correlation with Repair and a small negative association with Depression. The remaining Extrinsic measures exhibited one or more connections with psychological dysfunction, with Insecurity having especially negative mental health implications.

With the American data, partialing out the Intrinsic Scale removed the positive Religious Dependent Self correlation with Repair and the negative relationship with Depression. New associations of this factor also appeared with Anxiety (.22), Perceived Stress (.26), and Self- Esteem (–.16). Additional linkages emerged for Prayer and Practice with Externally Oriented Thinking (.15) and Self-Esteem (–.17); for Fear of God with Clarity (–.14), Anxiety (.14), and Perceived Stress (.22); and for E–P with Perceived Stress (.19, $ps < .05$). A number of zero-order correlations for the E–R items were eliminated, including direct associations with

TABLE 5
Correlations of Personal Negative Factors and Religious Orientation Measures With
Alexithymia, Emotional Intelligence, and Mental Health in the American Sample

Psychological Measures	Religious Measures							
	RDS	INS	PP	FG	INT	E–P	E–S	E–R
Alexithymia								
Difficulty Identifying Feelings	–.08	.20**	.15*	.02	–.15*	–.04	.09	.17*
Difficulty Describing Feelings	–.04	.09	.03	–.02	–.12	–.03	.02	.09
Externally Oriented Thinking	.02	.23**	.12	.22**	–.06	.15*	.16*	.19**
Emotional Intelligence								
Attention	.01	–.07	.01	–.09	.05	.03	–.08	–.10
Clarity	.06	–.21**	–.14*	–.06	.21**	.00	–.14*	–.21**
Repair	.14*	–.13*	–.04	.05	.37***	.07	–.15*	–.21**
Mental Health								
Anxiety	.12	.26***	.22**	.10	–.09	.09	.06	.17*
Depression	–.15*	.20**	.04	–.03	–.33***	–.03	.10	.22**
Perceived Stress	.05	.24***	.21**	.13	–.23**	.11	.09	.25***
Self–Esteem	.10	–.21**	–.08	.05	.34***	.08	–.05	–.16*

Note. Personal Negative Factors are Religion Dependent Self (RDS), Insecurity (INS), Prayer and Practice (PP), and Fear of God (FG). Religious Orientation measures are the Intrinsic Scale (INT), the Extrinsic–Personal (E–P) and Extrinsic–Social (E–S) factors, and the Extrinsic–Residual items.
$*p < .05. **p < .01. ***p < .001.$

Difficulty Identifying Feelings and Depression and inverse connections with Clarity, Repair, and Self-Esteem. These and other partial correlations confirmed that E–R items defined variance in a maladjusted anti-intrinsicness that was accounted for by the Intrinsic Scale. In all other partial correlations, no significant relationships were reversed from positive to negative, or vice versa, nor were any other nonsignificant outcomes transformed into significant associations, or vice versa.

Multiple regressions assessed the incremental validity of the Personal–Negative Scale by entering all four of its components into the second step of a regression equation after the Intrinsic, E–P, E–S, and E–R measures had been entered in on the first step. Few findings of incremental validity were evident in the Iranian sample. Prayer and Practice was a reliable predictor of Reflective Self-Knowledge ($\beta = -.24, p < .05$), as was Insecurity of Repair ($\beta = -.22, p < .05$). With the Americans, however, each Personal–Negative factor displayed at least some evidence of incremental validity. Associations appeared between the Religious Dependent Self factor and Difficulty Identifying Feelings ($\beta = -.26, p < .05$) and between Fear of God and Externally Oriented Thinking ($\beta = .26, p < .01$). Prayer and Practice displayed linkages with Anxiety (β = .21, p < .05) and Difficulty Identifying Feelings (β = .31, p < .01). Consistent evidence of incremental validity appeared for Insecurity with seven significant associations observed: Self-Reflectiveness (β = .27, p < .01), Anxiety (β = .23, p < .05), Depression (β = .28, p < .01), Self-Esteem (β = −.32, p < .01), Difficulty Identifying Feelings (β = .32, p < .01), Externally Oriented Thinking (β = .19, p < .05), and Clarity (β = −.19, p < .05).

In each sample separately, religious orientation measures were combined in a principal components analysis that used a varimax rotation. Table 6 demonstrates that two similar dimensions were obtained in both cultures. The first was a general religious motivation component that was defined by primary (i.e., strongest) or noteworthy secondary (i.e., > .30) loadings by all religious orientation variables except for the E–R items. The second component was a bipolar Intrinsic dimension anchored by E–R at one end and by the Intrinsic Scale at the other.

Examination of all religious variables with a MANOVA revealed significant culture, F (8, 432) = 24.63, p < .001, but not gender nor culture × gender interaction, F's (8, 423)< 1.81, ps > .05 effects. With regard to the cultural differences, Americans displayed higher average responses per item on the Intrinsic Scale (M +/− SEM: 2.25 +/− 0.04) than did the Iranians (2.06 +/− 0.04), F (1, 439) = 10.10, p < .01]. Iranians scored higher on four other measures: Religion Dependent Self (1.64 +/− 0.04 vs. 1.43 +/− 0.05), Insecurity (1.60 +/− 0.05 vs. 0.92 +/− 0.05), Fear of God (1.60 +/− 0.05 vs. 1.34 +/− 0.05), and E–S (1.09 +/− 0.05 vs. 0.89 +/− 0.05), F's (1, 439) > 4.14, ps < .01.

TABLE 6
Factors Obtained With Religious Orientation Measures in Samples
From Iran and the United States

	Iran		United States	
Measure	1	2	1	2
Allport and Ross Measures				
Intrinsic	.73	−.42	.74	−.50
Extrinsic–Personal (E–P)	.82	−.26	.67	.29
Extrinsic–Social (E–S)	.57	.35	.32	.68
Extrinsic–Residual (E–R)	.02	.91	−.16	.89
Personal Negative Factors				
Religion Dependent Self	.89	−.05	.89	−.04
Insecurity	.81	.08	.46	.68
Prayer and Practice	.85	.15	.70	.42
Fear of God	.86	.13	.72	.25
Factor Statistics				
Eigenvalue	4.43	1.24	3.47	1.92
%Variance Explained	55.36%	15.49%	43.38%	24.03%

Note. Maximum loading for each variable is underlined. These data reflected use of a principal components analysis with a varimax rotation.

DISCUSSION

Factor analysis of the Personal–Negative Scale uncovered four dimensions of negatively reinforcing personal reasons for maintaining religious commitments. The largest Religious Dependent Self factor recorded reliance upon religion in order to avoid psychological vulnerabilities and a sense of moral inadequacy. The special importance of religion in efforts to overcome extreme meaninglessness and insecurity was demonstrated by the Insecurity factor. The Prayer and Practice component most notably recorded the use of prayer to eliminate personal misery and unhappiness. The final factor described a Fear of God that motivated religious activities. In Iran and the United States, correlations with religious orientation, inner awareness, and mental health confirmed the cross-cultural validity of these factors and of concepts associated with the Allportian research tradition.

In both cultures, Personal–Negative factors displayed consistent positive associations with the Intrinsic, E–P, and E–S measures. Religious Dependent Self linkages with the Intrinsic Scale were especially strong, and correlations once again confirmed that Intrinsic and Extrinsic religious motivations were not incompatible (Kirkpatrick, 1989; Pargament, 1992). At the same time, numerous findings suggested a stronger integration of these motivations in Iran. A direct association appeared between Insecurity and the Intrinsic Scale only in Iran. E–R items essentially reflected an "anti-intrinsicness," and the inverse E–R linkage with the Intrinsic Scale was less robust in the Iranians. In the United States, but not Iran, the Insecurity, Prayer and Practice, Fear of God, and E–S variables correlated directly with E–R, suggesting a greater polarization of American religious motivations in that these forms of extrinsicness were congruent with an anti-intrinsicness. In contrast, E–P correlated inversely with E–R in Iran, but not the United States. This outcome identified E–P as an "anti–anti-intrinsicness," again suggesting a greater compatibility between extrinsicness and intrinsicness in Iran. Finally, in the factor analyses, the anti-intrinsicness of E–R was more discriminable from extrinsicness in Iran than in the United States, a phenomenon observed previously (Ghorbani, Watson, Ghramaleki, Morris, & Hood, 2002). Again, these findings indicated that Intrinsic and Extrinsic motivations were more polarized in America and more integrated in Iran.

Taken together, these data suggested that a culture like Iran, in which social and institutional structures are formally organized in religious terms (e.g., Tamadonfar, 2001), may encourage a stronger assimilation of instrumental and non-instrumental reasons for being religious. Other social and religious factors may be important as well. The Qur'an encourages believers to overcome the challenges of life through energetic personal efforts ("Women," verse 71, p. 110; "The Spoils," verse 60, p. 204; "The Night Journey, " verse 12, p. 303; Arberry, 1955). It also emphasizes that those who forget God will experience difficulties ("Taha," verse 124, p. 348) and that God is wholly sufficient for those who trust in him ("Di-

vorce," verses 2-3, p. 284; "Abraham," verse 12, p. 275). Islam, therefore, pro-
motes an active and organized response to the problems of life that may appear to
be "extrinsic," but that also is grounded in an "intrinsic" reliance upon God. Iran is
a developing religious society with major economic problems. Economic problems may encourage Muslims to turn to God, and a turn to God may encourage
Muslims to use their faith in coping with personal economic problems. Intrinsic
and extrinsic motivations may exist in a dynamic interaction, as Muslim religion
supplies "concepts and technologies for the ordering of" both the inner and the
outer life.

This cultural contrast also might be described from an opposite perspective.
Secularization may promote a polarization of Intrinsic and Extrinsic motivations
as the institutional, economic, and other social rewards for maintaining sincere religious beliefs increasingly decline. Positive associations of the anti-intrinsicness
of E–R with Insecurity, Prayer and Practice, Fear of God, and E–S in the United
States but not in Iran would exemplify this greater polarization within a more secularized society. Of course, such cultural differences might simply reflect differences in specific Muslim and Christian beliefs, since contrasting beliefs
undoubtedly have many important effects. Still, correlations of Muslim beliefs
with personality in Great Britain (Wilde & Joseph, 1997) differ from those observed in Iran in a manner suggesting that secularization may be a more plausible
explanation (Ghorbani, Watson, Ghramaleki, Morris, & Hood, 2000).

Even clearer cross-cultural dissimilarities appeared in the Self-Consciousness
and Self-Knowledge data. The Personal–Negative and other religious orientation
measures consistently predicted higher values on these variables in Iran but not in
the United States. Such contrasts were not explicable in terms of the adjustment
implications of the constructs. In Iran – as in the United States–Internal State
Awareness, Experiential Self-Knowledge, and Reflective Self-Knowledge have
predicted adaptive functioning, whereas Self-Reflectiveness and Social Anxiety
have correlated with psychological dysfunction (Ghorbani, Bing, Watson,
Davison, & LeBreton, 2002; Watson et al., 1994, 1996). Nor was the difference attributable to some unknown anomalous feature of this particular American sample. Earlier studies using students from the same state university have uncovered
similar nonexistent or very small religious orientation relationships with
Self-Consciousness (Watson, Morris, Foster, & Hood, 1986; Watson, Morris, &
Hood, 1988a, 1988b).

Instead, these cultural differences perhaps revealed that life in a more formally
religious society promoted not only a stronger integration among religious motivations, but also a stronger integration of religious motivations with personal understandings of the self. Perhaps supporting this possibility was an earlier observation
that even in the United States, students from a Pentecostal Christian college (and
thus presumably from a more religious, less "secularized" background) displayed
Intrinsic ties with Internal State Awareness (.48) and Style Consciousness (.36)

that were as strong as those obtained with this Iranian sample (Watson et al., 1988a).

Relationships with the other inner awareness variables further confirmed that Muslim religion supplied "concepts and technologies for the ordering of the inner life." They also established that point for the Americans. With regard to Alexithymia, six Extrinsic measures in Iran and three in the United States predicted greater Difficulty Identifying Feelings. In Iran, the Religion Dependent Self and Insecurity factors also correlated positively with Difficulty Describing Feelings. Data for Externally Oriented Thinking were more complex. Insecurity, Fear of God, E–P, E–S, and E–R displayed direct associations with Externally Oriented Thinking in the United States; but in Iran, the Religion Dependent Self factor and E–P exhibited counterintuitive inverse linkages with Externally Oriented Thinking. However, the Intrinsic Scale correlated negatively with Externally Oriented Thinking in Iran and with Difficulty Identifying Feelings in the United States, and the Extrinsic data became less ambiguous in partial correlations controlling for intrinsicness. In the Iranian partial correlations, for example, the negative Religion Dependent Self relationship with Externally Oriented Thinking became significant in the positive direction, the inverse E–P connection with this aspect of Alexithymia became nonsignificant, and numerous new direct associations appeared between the Extrinsic and Alexithymia variables. In both samples, therefore, extrinsicness reflected greater deficits in the processing of emotional information whereas the opposite was true of intrinsicness.

Further support for this conclusion came in the examination of Emotional Intelligence. Linkages of the Intrinsic Scale with greater Clarity and Repair were obvious in both cultures. As with Alexithymia, ambiguities appeared in the zero-order Extrinsic relationships, but with one exception, partialing out the Intrinsic Scale once again identified extrinsicness as a correlate of maladjusted emotional processing. The one exception occurred in the Iranian sample and involved the diminished, but still significant positive partial correlation of E–P with Repair. This outcome perhaps supplied the clearest, though weak evidence that an Extrinsic motivation may at least sometimes have influences that are more favorable than Allport imagined (Pargament, 1992).

Zero-order and partial correlations with mental health supplied a final line of evidence in favor of the Allportian characterization of religious orientation. Intrinsic relationships were nearly identical across the two samples with this scale predicting greater Self-Esteem and lower Depression and Perceived Stress. In the less ambiguous partial correlations controlling for the Intrinsic Scale, Extrinsic measures were associated with lower Self-Esteem and greater Anxiety, Depression, and Perceived Stress.

Beyond correlating with personality and with the other religious orientation variables, the new Personal–Negative measures demonstrated their utility in a number of additional ways. First, multiple regressions established that these negatively reinforcing reasons for being religious had incremental validity. Each component yielded at least one outcome documenting that it explained variance not accounted for by the Allport and Ross constructs. Insecurity proved to be particularly noteworthy in The United States. It was a reliable contributor to seven prediction equations. In Iran, Insecurity displayed only an inverse association with Repair. The reason for this cross-cultural contrast was not clear, but one possibility was that Americans read these items differently than Iranians. This component included phrases like "I try to believe…" and "I try to follow…." Within the context of being insecure, such statements in English may more likely connote a kind of desperation in which the implication is that "I try but seem unable to believe or to follow…" This possible difference might again reflect the secularization issue. Life in a more secularized culture might make attempts to use religion for such purposes seem more desperate.

Indeed, at a higher level of abstraction, multiple regressions may have supplied additional evidence of the importance of cultural differences in secularization. In Iran, only two findings testified in favor of the incremental validity of the Personal–Negative Scale. In the United States, 11 results confirmed such a conclusion. A stronger assimilation among religious motivations presumably would increase the likelihood that only a subset could fully explain religious linkages with inner awareness and mental health. The Allport and Ross variables, in other words, perhaps offered a more nearly sufficient accounting of individual differences in religious commitments under conditions of greater integration. Cultural contrasts in the incremental validity data, therefore, may have further revealed a stronger integration of religious motivations in Iran.

Personal–Negative components also proved to be useful in factor analyses examining all of the religious orientation measures. In both cultures, two factors emerged. These dimensions did not describe Allport's differentiation between Intrinsic and Extrinsic orientations. Instead, they defined a general religious motivation factor and a bipolar Intrinsic dimension. Roughly the same outcome was observed previously (Ghorbani, Watson, Ghramaleki, Morris, & Hood, 2002), and thus seemed to be reliable. Loadings of Intrinsic and Extrinsic measures on the same factor again supported claims that the two motivations can be compatible (Pargament, 1992). Zero-order and partial correlations nevertheless demonstrated that the Intrinsic dimension was more important in predicting positive mental health. In addition, partial correlations in both cultures, but particularly in Iran, suggested that intrinsicness ameliorated the maladjusted psychological implications of extrinsicness.

Finally, use of the Personal–Negative factors resulted in a more detailed analysis of mean cultural differences in religious orientation. Iranians displayed higher scores on the Religion Dependent Self, Insecurity, and Fear of God factors, as well as on E–S, but not E–P. The cross-cultural difference in E–S perhaps supplied an additional indication that Iran was less secularized. Without the Personal–Negative

Scale, however, the misleading conclusion would have been that cultural differences in extrinsicness were limited to the social aspects of religion. The Personal–Negative data helped avoid this misinterpretation and thereby further proved the utility of this new instrument. Moreover, this investigation only sought to establish the basic and incremental validity of the Personal–Negative Scale. While some evidence for incremental validity was limited, especially in Iran, the availability of this instrument now makes it possible to move beyond scale development considerations. For instance, could Extrinsic associations with maladjustment be wholly or largely attributable to negatively reinforcing personal reasons for being religious? This is a plausible hypothesis with important theoretical and perhaps even clinical implications that the Personal–Negative Scale now makes it possible to test.

Of all the findings of this project, the most unexpected was the cultural difference in the Intrinsic Scale. Americans scored higher. This outcome was not obtained in the previous examination of these two cultures, although Americans did surprisingly express nonsignificantly higher levels of an interest in religion (Ghorbani, Watson, Ghramaleki, Morris, & Hood, 2002). Only in the present investigation, however, was the internal reliability of the Intrinsic Scale improved by dropping two items, and this procedure may have explained the difference. In addition, previous samples of similar Americans have displayed noteworthy variations in religious commitments that had important effects on empirical findings (Watson, Morris, & Hood, 1989). The present American sample may simply have been more religious than the one examined in the previous Iranian–American study. More generally, these students lived in a part of the United States that is well known for stronger and more conservative religious beliefs. Observation of this cultural difference might have been less likely with subjects from a different part of the United States. Finally, this outcome perhaps supplied further evidence of secularization. For those who are able to maintain commitments in a more secularized environment, Intrinsic motivations for being religious may need to be stronger and more compelling.

In conclusion, this project has already made it clear that Allport's approach to religion cannot be limited to intracultural Christian concerns (McCrae, 2001). True, factor analysis in both samples failed to describe religious orientation in terms of Allport's Intrinsic–Extrinsic dichotomy. Some findings also revealed that extrinsicness at least sometimes predicted positive psychological functioning. More often than not, however, intrinsicness was associated with adjustment whereas extrinsicness was more indicative of maladjustment, just as Allport would have expected. The negative mental health implications of extrinsicness often became clear only after partial correlations controlled for intrinsicness. Such partial correlations, therefore, documented that unambiguous understandings of religious motivation and mental health require a theoretical and empirical sensitivity to Allport's insights. Of course, no single study can prove that the Intrinsic-Extrinsic distinction will support a broad-based intercultural and transcultural research program in the psychology of religion. In addition, the lower internal reliabilities of some extrinsic measures suggested that further refinements might be necessary in some of the measuring instruments. Still, these data demonstrated that an Allportian perspective currently supplies a productive conceptual framework for conducting cross-cultural studies in the psychology of religion and that Personal–Negative constructs may usefully supplement other religious orientation variables in such investigations.

ACKNOWLEDGMENTS

A version of this study was presented at the XIVth Conference of the International Association for Psychology of Religion at Soesterberg in the Netherlands in September 2001. The support of Mr. Mohammad Ali Mahdavi, Head of the General Office of Managerial Affairs in Tehran, Iran, is gratefully acknowledged.

REFERENCES

Allport, G. W. (1950). *The individual and his religion.* New York: Macmillan.

Allport, G. W., & Ross, J. M. (1967). Religious orientation and prejudice. *Journal of Personality and Social Psychology, 5,* 432–443.

Arberry, A. J. (Trans.). (1955). *The Koran interpreted.* Touchstone: New York.

Bagby, R. M., Parker, J. D. A., & Taylor, G. J. (1994). The twenty-item Toronto Alexithymia Scale — I. Item selection and cross-validation of the factor structure. *Journal of Psychosomatic Research, 38,* 23–32.

Bagby, R. M., Taylor, G. J., & Parker, D. D. (1994). The twenty-item Toronto Alexithymia Scale — II. Convergent, discriminant, and concurrent validity. *Journal of Psychosomatic Research, 38,* 33–40.

Browning, D. S. (1987). *Religious thought and the modern psychologies.* Philadelphia: Fortress.

Calvin, J. (1960). *Institutes of the Christian religion.* Philadelphia: Westminster Press. (Original work published 1559)

Chang, E. C. (1998). Does dispositional optimism moderate the relation between perceived stress and psychological well-being? A preliminary investigation. *Personality and Individual Differences, 25,* 233–240.

Cohen, S., Kamarck, T., & Mermelstein, R. A. (1983). A global measure of perceived stress. *Journal of Health and Social Psychology, 24,* 355–396.

Costello, C. G., & Comrey, A. L. (1967). Scales for measuring depression and anxiety. *Journal of Psychology, 66,* 303–313.

Donahue, M. J. (1985). Intrinsic and extrinsic religiousness: Review and meta-analysis. *Journal of Personality and Social Psychology, 48,* 400–419.

Fenigstein, A., Scheier, M. F., & Buss, A. H. (1975). Public and private self-consciousness: Assessment and theory. *Journal of Consulting and Clinical Psychology, 43,* 522–527.

Frozanfar, B. Z. (1991). *Ahadis masnavi* [Sayings of the Mathnawi] (5th ed.). Tehran: Amir Kabir. (Original work published in 1370)

Ghorbani, N., Bing, M. N., Watson, P. J., Davison, H. K., & Mack, D. A. (in press). Emotional intelligence in cross-cultural perspective: Construct similarity and functional dissimilarity in higher order processing in Iran and the United States. *International Journal of Psychology.*

Ghorbani, N., Watson, P. J., Bing, M. N., Davison, H. K., & LeBreton, D. L. (2002). *Two facets of self-knowledge: Cross-cultural analysis of a new conceptualization in Iran and the United States.* Manuscript in preparation.

Ghorbani, N., Watson, P. J., Ghramaleki, A. F., Morris, R. J., & Hood, R. W., Jr. (2000). Muslim Attitudes towards Religion Scale: Factors, validity, and complexity of relationships with mental health in Iran. *Mental Health, Religion, and Culture, 3,* 125–132.

Ghorbani, N., Watson, P. J., Ghramaleki, A. F., Morris, R. J., & Hood, R. W., Jr. (2002). Muslim-Christian Religious Orientation Scales: Distinctions, correlations, and cross-cultural analysis in Iran and the United States. *The International Journal for the Psychology of Religion, 12,* 73–95.

Hood, R. W., Jr., Spilka, B., Hunsberger, B., & Gorsuch, R. (1996). *The psychology of religion* (2nd ed.). New York: Guilford.

Khansari, S. J. (1987). *Sharhe dorar va dorar Amedi* [Persian explanation of Amedi's Ghorar and Dorar]. Tehran: University of Tehran. (Original work published in 1366)

Kirkpatrick, L. A. (1989). A psychometric analysis of the Allport-Ross and Feagan measures of intrinsic-extrinsic religious orientation. In D. O. Moberg & M. L. Lynn (Eds.), *Research in the Social Scientific Study of Religion* (Vol. 1, pp. 1–30). Greenwich, CT: JAI.

McCrae, R. R. (2001). Trait psychology and culture: Exploring intercultural comparisons. *Journal of Personality, 69,* 819–846.

Mittal, B., & Balasubramanian, S. K. (1987). Testing the dimensionality of the self- consciousness scales. *Journal of Personality Assessment, 51,* 53–68.

Pargament, K. I. (1992). Of means and ends: Religion and the search for significance. *The International Journal for the Psychology of Religion, 2,* 201–229.

Parker, J. D. A., Taylor, G. J., & Bagby, M. (2001). The relationship between emotional intelligence and alexithymia. *Personality and Individual Differences, 30,* 107–115.

Robinson, J. P., & Shaver, P. R. (1973). *Measures of social and psychological attitudes* (Revised edition). Ann Arbor, MI: Institute for Social Research.

Rosenberg, M. (1965). *Society and adolescent self-image.* Princeton, NJ: Princeton University.

Salovey, P., Mayer, J. D., Goldman, S. L., Turvey, C., & Palfai, T. P. (1995). Emotional attention, clarity, and repair: Exploring emotional intelligence using the trait meta-mood scale. In J. W. Pennebaker (Ed.), *Emotion, disclosure, & health* (pp. 125–154). Washington, DC: American Psychological Association.

Tamadonfar, M. (2001). Islam, law, and political control in contemporary Iran. *Journal for the Scientific Study of Religion, 40,* 203–219.

Watson, P. J., Hickman, S. E., Morris, R. J., Stutz, N. L., & Whiting, L. (1994). Complexity of self-consciousness subscales: correlations of factors with self-esteem and dietary restraint. *Journal of Social Behavior and Personality, 9,* 761–774.

Watson, P. J., Morris, R. J., Foster, J. E., & Hood, R. W., Jr. (1986). Religiosity and social desirability. *Journal for the Scientific Study of Religion, 25,* 215–232.

Watson, P. J., Morris, R. J., Hood, R. W., Jr. (1988a). Sin and self-functioning, Part 1: Grace, guilt, and self-consciousness. *Journal of Psychology and Theology, 16,* 254–269.

Watson, P. J., Morris, R. J., Hood, R. W., Jr. (1988b). Sin and self-functioning, Part 2: Grace, guilt, and psychological adjustment. *Journal of Psychology and Theology, 16,* 270–281.

Watson, P. J., Morris, R. J., Hood, R. W., Jr. (1989). Sin and self-functioning, Part 4: Depression, assertiveness, and religious commitments. *Journal of Psychology and Theology, 17,* 44–58.

Watson, P. J., Morris, R. J., Ramsey, A., Hickman, S. E., & Waddell, M. G. (1996). Further contrasts between self-reflectiveness and internal state awareness factors of private self- consciousness. *Journal of Psychology, 130,* 183–192.

Wilde, A., & Joseph, S. (1997). Religiosity and personality in a Moslem context. *Personality and Individual Differences, 23,* 899–900.

THE INTERNATIONAL JOURNAL FOR THE PSYCHOLOGY OF RELIGION, *12*(4), 277–289

PERSPECTIVE

Religious Psychology in Malaysia

Amber Haque and Khairol A. Masuan

Department of Psychology
International Islamic University Malaysia

The growth of religious psychology with specific reference to the Malay people as the majority culture is discussed. This article describes attitudes of the Malays toward religion, and reviews related programs and developments in Malaysian universities and institutes. It covers contents of major seminars and conferences held in recent years; the application of religious psychology in the general Malay population and an analysis of some problems and prospects relevant to the general psychology of religion area. The article concludes that, although psychology of religion does not exist here in the Western sense, immense opportunities exist for psychological research on religion. Suggestions for improving the psychology–religion interface are given.

Malaysia is comprised of three main ethnic groups, the Malays, the Chinese and the Indians. Malays are the indigenous people of Malaysia, with a majority population exceeding 50%. They are also known as *Bumiputras* or "sons of the soil". The Malaysian Constitution declares Islam as the official religion of the country, but other religions are given freedom of practice. Malays were originally Hindus and practiced animism prior to fourteenth century, after which they embraced Islam. Among Malaysians, and especially the Malays, the traditional belief that spiritual forces play a great role over physical and mental health is dominant. The British colonialists brought Chinese and Indians into Malaysia in the nineteenth century. A substantial portion of the Chinese population claim affiliation with Christianity and Buddhism; the Hindus have an even more diverse belief system. Within the Malay population, there are also cultural differences from state to state but the overall Ma-

Requests for reprints can be addressed to Amber Haque, Department of Psychology, International Islamic University, Jalan Gombak, 53100 Kuala Lumpur, Malaysia. E-mail: amberhaque@yahoo.com

lay culture is overshadowed by a strong influence of religion. This article covers religious psychology within the Malay context and culture, simply because of the unavailability of data for the minority religious groups. It is hard to find Chinese and Hindu psychologists in Malaysian universities, and published works in the area of psychology and religion are currently not available from the minority religions. It also needs to be pointed out, at the outset, that psychology of religion does not exist as an independent area of study in Malaysian universities in the departments of psychology, as only 3 out of 17 universities in the country have this department. This figure should give the readers a clue to the status of psychology as a discipline in Malaysia. Religious psychology, on the other hand, is pervasive in all walks of life among the Malaysians, whether they are Muslims, Christians, Buddhists, or Hindus. These groups have a long-standing association with religious institutions. This is in contrast to a significant population in The United States, which describes itself as "spiritual but not religious" meaning that they are not associated with a traditional religious institution (Hoge, 1996).

ATTITUDE TOWARD RELIGION

Religion plays a significant role in the lives of the Malays. Azhar (2001) wrote that over the past 15 years, there has been a religious awareness taking place among the Malays, resulting in a religious revival in this country. Although no study is presently available, looking at the practices of the local people, one could estimate that 90% or more of the Malay population is generally seen as practicing their basic beliefs of Islam. Muslims in general, including the Malays, view religion as superior to scientific analysis and do not question Islamic principles laid down in the Qur'an, the Muslim holy book. The Muslim belief is primarily based on the idea that one cannot separate science from religion, as both work in an integrated whole as a part of cosmic reality. Human beings are considered a microcosm of the larger cosmos; demonstrating the affinity between humans and nature and the common elements that exist between them. Rahman (1989) pointed out that when God creates something, He puts into it its nature and the law that governs it, whereby it falls into a pattern and becomes a part of the total cosmos. Although objects of nature—like the sun, the moon, and the stars—have no choice but to act according to God's laws, human beings, in contrast, are given a (limited) choice to follow or not to follow the commands of God. The reward and punishment in the hereafter is based on actions that are consistent with or against the commands of God given in the Qur'an. The seat of true knowledge in human beings comes from the metaphysical elements, referred to in the Qur'an as heart (*qalb*), soul (*al-nafs*), spirit (*ruh*), and intellect (*al-aql*). Knowledge and *ruh* are inherent in the nature of human beings and are collectively known as *al-fitrah*, which directs human behavior throughout their lives. Deviation from *al-fitrah* leads humans to go astray and leads to suffering and pains in this world.

A Muslim is duty-bound to unravel the mysteries of nature not only through speculation and science, but also through the divine words and attained wisdom, by reflecting on the verses of Qur'an. In Islam, and among certain Muslim intellectuals, there is a growing interest in integrating science and religion and viewing all phenomena of life, including human behavior, from this perspective. Faruqi (1995) started the Islamization of Knowledge (IOK) project, which refers to processes that are utilized to construct and recast the total corpus of human knowledge so that it conforms to the key concept in Islam, *al-Tawhid* (Unity or Oneness of God). Syed Naquib Al-Attas, founder-director of the International Institute of Islamic Thought and Civilization (ISTAC) an academic research institute in Kuala Lumpur, Malaysia, is credited for laying the theoretical foundation of the IOK, while Faruqi's contribution is more on the methodological side. The IOK approach calls for making all knowledge subservient to, and in consonance with, the entire cosmic laws derived from the teachings of the Qur'an. This attitude of Muslim social scientists has led to numerous researches and findings of a direct influence of religion on human behavior. The efforts of Faruqi and Al-Attas are reflected in many burgeoning institutions around the Muslim world, prominent among which is the International Islamic University of Malaysia.

MALAYSIAN UNIVERSITIES

The first department of psychology was established at the *Universiti Kebangsaan Malaysia* (UKM) in the 1970s. Although the department is not Islamically oriented, the faculty members are mainly Muslims trained in the West. There is no psychology of religion course as such, but because of an Islamic influence on the culture, secular psychology is often evaluated from Islamic perspective. Certain faculty members have published works depicting the influence of religion on behavior. Salleh (1993) from UKM wrote about the virtues of *Dhikr* (ritual chanting) on health. Although, *Dhikr* is an Islamic term and would comprehensively mean God- consciousness, Salleh uses the term "mantras" which are utterances of poetic nature and contain a magical connotation. Rituals such as chanting are the influences of Hinduism on Malay culture. For the Sufis, *Dhikr* is a spiritual method of remembering God, often used as a sacred formula given to the disciple from the *Shaykh* or the spiritual master.

The Department of Islamic Studies at UKM offers religious treatment for psychological disorders through *Darul Shifa* (treatment center) using Islamic principles of counseling. Treatment fee is not mandatory and depends upon the client's ability to pay. In Malay belief, the payment for religious services is considered a commitment on behalf of the client, rather than a payment for service offered, and is called *Pengeras*. The head of *Darul Shifa*, Dr. Harun Din is widely regarded as a spiritual healer and the one who uses various transcendental methods including invocating the *Jinns* (Genie). The existence of *Jinns* is mentioned in the Qur'an and sometimes humans and *Jinns* are addressed together (see, e.g., Philips, 1996). The belief in possession by unseen forces is common among Muslims and especially in the Malay culture. The Department of Psychiatry at UKM has also shown considerable interest in the influence of religious beliefs on client's mental health. Shahrom Hatta published a book on *Psychological Medicine in Islam* (1995) and other relevant articles (1998, 2001) that attempt to put the nature of psychological disorders in proper Islamic and Malay cultural contexts.

The establishment of the International Islamic University Malaysia (IIUM) in Kuala Lumpur in 1983 and its Human Sciences Faculty in 1990 was the beginning of a new era in integrative studies, at least in this part of the world. IIUM is the outcome of a conference on education in the Muslim world organized by Saudi Arabia in Mecca in 1977. Dr. Mahathir Mohammad, Prime Minister of Malaysia, implemented the idea of an international university emphasizing integrative education, and the university grew from a mere couple of hundred students in 1983 to over 16,000 in year 2001. International Muslim scholars joined the university and showed great enthusiasm over this project, especially in the social science departments. Malik Badri from Sudan joined the department of psychology in 1992 and was the first member of the faculty to introduce Islam and Psychology course at the undergraduate level. Badri's book, *The Dilemma of Muslim Psychologists* published in 1979, critically examines contemporary psychological theories and asks whether a theory of human behavior is possible while rejecting the concept of human soul. Badri urges Muslim psychologists to look into their past and acknowledge the contributions of early Muslim scholars like Ghazali, Ibn Qayim, Ibn Khaldun and Ibn Sireen in the areas of human nature, cognitive therapy, social psychology and dream analysis. The dilemma for Muslim psychologists is whether they should emulate the line of their ancestors or join mainstream psychology, elements of which run contrary to Islamic beliefs. Badri recommends that Muslim psychologists need to utilize the methodology of modern psychology without taking the underlying metaphysics. For example, while he rejects the philosophy behind behaviorism, he accepts the use of behavioral techniques in treatment of clients because he equates such treatment to a value-free mechanical activity. He cites cases where he found recitation of the Qur'an extremely helpful in changing client's outlook on life; especially when mainstream psychology had minimum or no beneficial effect upon the client. Badri left IIUM in 1994 and joined ISTAC, from where he published several works related to the area of psychology and religion. His recent book, *Contemplation: A Psychospiritual Study* (2000) talks about developing a religious outlook on life as a means of coping, and a basis of fostering happiness. Badri refers to several recent studies in the neurosciences, which validates his arguments, that is, the need to integrate science and religion.

The IIUM Department of Psychology boasts other members, from around the world, who have a keen interest in psychology and religion. Zafar Afaq Ansari, who headed the National Institute of Pakistan in Islamabad, joined IIUM in 1992 as well. He published an edited book entitled *Qur'anic Concepts of Human Psyche* (1992) and became the first editor of *Intellectual Discourse*, a journal of the Human Sciences Faculty at IIUM, which publishes social science articles from a religious perspective. Ansari's book explains the meaning of psyche in Islamic Gnostic and philosophical tradition. Special emphasis is given to the concept of soul and to the heart as the locus of the human psyche. Mental health and measurement of religiosity from an Islamic perspective are also covered. The book presents a challenge to Muslim psychologists to study human nature from various Qur'anic perspectives, as it is full of examples, terminologies, and metaphors that explain the intricacies of human personality. Abbas Hussein Ali from Sudan published a paper in English in 1995, and others in Arabic while he worked at IIUM between 1992 and 1995. His article is a summary of Ghazali's contribution to personality theory, derived primarily from the Qur'an. Quazi Shamsuddin Ilyas from Bangladesh taught here from 1994 to 1996, and proposed in Ansari's book the development of a Muslim Religiosity Scale, emphasizing the use of *taqwa* (God consciousness) to signify religiosity and use it as a multi-dimensional variable with the assumption that these different dimensions are related to one another. Although serious attempts have been made to construct and adapt psychological tests for use in Muslim cultures, the results are generally poor. Perhaps Egypt is the only exception where psychology grew over the years and psychological assessments including religiosity scales in Arabic have been developed and used in the neighboring Arab countries. Construction of psychological tests needs experts, which are rare in Muslim countries, and Malaysia is no exception. Furthermore, the process is a long and tedious one, and the ongoing support structure for such activities is generally lacking. A bigger problem, however, is a lack of Islamic psychological paradigm that would guide Muslim psychologists in their endeavors to "Islamize" their discipline.

After Badri left in 1994, the Islam and Psychology course was taught by people from different countries, like Abbas Hussein Ali (Sudan), Nizar Al-Ani (Iraq), Mustapha Achoui (Algeria), Khairol Anuar Masuan (Malaysia), Shamsur Rehman Khan (India), Alizi Alias (Malaysia) and later Djilali Bouhmama (Algeria), Mohamad Mokdad (Algeria), and Shukran Abdur Rahman (Malaysia) in turns, because many international staff left the department at the end of their contracts for personal reasons. Although the turnover of faculty members has been high, the presence of members from different countries shows the international character of the university in general, and the department in particular. Al-Ani completed a translation of his master's thesis on the psychology of personality from an Islamic perspective, but then left IIUM in 1998. Achoui published his article comparing Western dimensions of human nature with Islamic perspective in a special issue of the *American Journal of Islamic Social Sciences* in 1998 devoted to psychology. This was perhaps necessary, as Achoui taught a personality course using a textbook, with Western approaches, which covered contemporary theories from a "scientific" point of view, and this did not satisfy the integrated model which IIUM propagates. Sole dependence on the secular approach is discouraged at IIUM, as it defeats the mission and vision of the university. Amber Haque joined the department in 1996 and published several articles on psychology and religion (Haque, 1996, 1998b, 1999, 2000, 2001a, 2001b, 2001c). Haque introduced Islamic perspectives in his Theories of Personality course. Special material based on the works of different Muslim scholars from around the world is currently being compiled as an edited book to serve as a supplementary text for this course. Haque also started a newsletter highlighting Islamic perspectives in psychology, which appeared for about two years (six issues) and was then terminated in 1998 due to lack of funds. This newsletter served as a vehicle for networking among Muslim psychologists in many countries. Language and cultural barriers, however, proved to be a problem for a more effective growth of the newsletter. The Department of Psychology has started the Islamization of Knowledge course, with special reference to psychology for master's level students. Proponents of IOK recommend that Muslim scholars be well versed in Islamic and other knowledge, in order to benefit from the integration of these approaches. However, there are critics of IOK who say that all knowledge is given by God and is thus already "Islamic." They argue that for IOK to take place, one has to "desecularize" knowledge, replacing it with ideas from the Qur'an. For them, a thorough knowledge of Qur'an is essential, and the mastering of other knowledge is of secondary importance. Because this debate is outside the scope of this article, only a passing remark is given here. Masters' theses granted by the psychology department at IIUM also focus on religiosity issues using either Western or adapted scales or a combination of both. Any reader would note the prevailing stance of religion, rather than that of psychological theories or research methodologies in these works as may be the case in the West. This approach is relatively less emphasized in other Malaysian universities, which generally follow the secular model of education.

RELIGIOUS INSTITUTES

There are institutes, as well, with interest in religious psychology, for example, ISTAC, *Institute Kefahaman Islam Malaysia* (IKIM), *Jabatan Kemajuan Islam Malaysia* (JAKIM), *Angkatan Belia Islam Malaysia* (ABIM), and *Jama'a Islah Malaysia* (JIM). Although ISTAC is a highly intellectually oriented institute of international standing, the other local institutes disseminate Islamic knowledge and services to the local population; and publish books, articles, and newsletters of religious nature. ISTAC's founder-director, Syed Naqib Al-Attas, has published several psychology-religion related manuscripts including *The Nature of Man and the Psychology of Human Soul* (1990), *Islam: The Concept of Religion and the Foundation of Ethics and Morality* (1992), *The Meaning and Experience of Happiness in*

Islam (1993), and *The Degrees of Existence* (1994), among others. The writings of Al-Attas focus on the classical perspectives of human nature, based on a dualistic dimension of body and soul, and seem to be highly influenced by the works of Ghazali and Ibn Sina. Discussions on psychology and religion issues are also quite evident from several master's theses of graduating students from ISTAC, as well as from the official publication of *Al-Shajarah*, the institute's intellectual journal. ISTAC has an outstanding collection of rare books in several languages in its library. The seriousness of ISTAC's stance on reviving Islamic thought is evident from these efforts, as well as from a recent international conference to celebrate Ghazali held in October 2001. Much of Ghazali's work is related to metaphysical aspects in psychology. The high quality and diverse international faculty at ISTAC attract many students into the postgraduate program.

The *Jabatan Agamah Islam Selangor* (JAIS) is a state level agency that provides Islamic counseling services for the public and even trains the *Imams* (religious leaders) in basic human psychology. The working members of JAIS are counseling professionals employed by the government. Whereas basic counselor training at the university level is done purely in the secular mode (except for IIUM), it is impressive how the Malays combine that knowledge with their cultural and religious values in treating their clients. Workshops and seminars are regularly arranged to deal with such issues, and are run by the counseling professionals as well as religious experts. The *Jabatan Perkhidmatan Awam* (JPA) is also a government-based agency headed by Maat Sat Baki, a Western trained clinical psychologist. JPA offers services from secular as well as religious perspectives. Baki (1993) discussed abnormal behaviors in Malay culture and the subtle but strong influence of religion on these people. Realizing the sentimental attachment of the Malay people to religion, psychologists and psychiatrists may also encourage clients to see spiritual healers simultaneously.

SEMINARS AND CONFERENCES

An International Seminar on Islamic Thought was held at UKM in 1984, organized by the International Institute of Islamic Thought (IIIT) and Ministry of Culture, Youth, and Sports. This seminar focused on all aspects of social science disciplines including psychology, and particularly Islamic psychology. Papers presented generally talked about structures of mind, consciousness and personality from an Islamic perspective. Unfortunately, the conference proceedings are not available to get a complete account of the deliberations of that conference.

A national and an international conference were organized by the Psychology Department, IIUM, with the aims of integrating psychology and religion (see Haque, 1977, 1998a). The main objective of the national conference, held in

1996, was to form a network of psychologists in Malaysia in order to develop an Islamic outlook on psychology, that is, to assess behavior and mental processes from the Qur'anic perspective. Related aims were also to learn the state of the art regarding Islamic psychology in Malaysia, evaluate efforts in curriculum changes (integrating science and religion), and planning for the future. A major concern of the conference was the lack of spiritual content taught in nonreligious schools, a dimension revered by religion and many cultures of the world. Papers were read on themes including the relationship between social sciences and religion, human nature from religious perspectives, faith as a prerequisite in "Islamizing" psychology, Islamic approach to psychopathology and counseling, and some theoretical contributions, for example a proposed Islamic theory of arousal and information processing. The conference ended with broad recommendations on developing an Islamic framework of psychology and showing how it is different from secular psychology; using the transcendental model as a guide for Muslim psychologists rather than the approach of "adaptability," and an appreciation of the interconnectedness of psychology with its sister disciplines. After 5 years of this conference, nothing conspicuous has been achieved, but efforts toward reaching its goals continue.

The International Conference on Counseling and Psychotherapy, held in 1997, presented further Qur'anic insights into psychotherapy, highlighted contributions of early Muslim scholars in counseling and psychotherapy, discussed human nature from Islamic perspective, and shared empirical studies on psychology and religion from Iran, Malaysia, Pakistan, Egypt, Saudi Arabia and the United States. Many other issues relevant to psychology and religion were also covered. The main theme of this conference was that most misunderstandings in psychology are created by incorrect assumptions of human nature, ranging from the Darwinian concept of human beings to the model of humans as an information processing unit, that entirely elude the spiritual dimension. The conference ended with the idea that quantification in psychology may be fascinating, but often leads to illusory knowledge, especially if the method of quantification is faulty, and thus psychology cannot do without metaphysics. What was noticeable in both conferences was that a majority of papers were theoretical in nature and very few were based on empirical studies. These lacunae exist because, first, Muslim psychologists are struggling to revive and design their own framework and philosophy of human nature, and second, there is a lack of indigenous psychological tests, which are imperative for any empirical investigation on local population. In a conference on Religion and Mental Health held in Iran in 2001 (see Khalili et al., this issue), there were far more empirical researches on religion than there were theoretical papers. This shows that Iranian psychologists are generally ahead of other Muslim psychologists from different countries in test construction and its use in the area of psychology and religion.

A smaller level conference entitled *Psychology: Towards Well-Being and Self-Actualization* was organized by the Malaysian Psychological Association and co-sponsored by the Department of Psychology (IIUM) in July 2001. Papers that were presented addressed the psychology-religion relationship, for example Islamic model of mental health and guidance (Watanabe, 2001); effect of prayer as a mode of reducing anxiety in Malay subjects awaiting open heart surgery in Malaysia (Khan, 2001); religiosity, values and social problems in Malaysia (Noon, 2001); selected works of early Muslim scholars on obsessive compulsive behavior: a comparative study (Asif, 2001), and the concept of *mau'izah* in Islamic counseling (Marzuki, Ahmad, & Ahmad, 2001). Although this conference was small, the number of empirical studies was higher as compared to papers presented in previous Malaysian conferences. This indicates a slow but steady growth in the empirical researches here.

Other universities with staff members having interest in psychology and religion are University of Malaya (UM), University Malaysia Sabah (UMS), and University Science Malaysia (USM). Abdul Halim Othman (1993) of UMS edited *Psikologi Melayu* (Malay Psychology), addressing the strong influence of culture on the Malays. However he reminds us that the Malay culture itself is highly influenced by the Islamic religion. Mohamad Zain Azhar from USM has written several papers on religious influence on psychiatric patients (1995, 1996, 1999, 2001). Azhar's papers are, by and large, empirical in nature and often address the culture-bound syndromes in different Malay groups.

APPLYING RELIGIOUS PSYCHOLOGY

In the Malay society, a *Kampung,* or village, generally has a *"Bomoh,"* or traditional healer, who helps clients with psychological disorders. Because mental illness is often considered a possession by the *Jinn* or spirit, and a stigma for the family, the inflicted person is taken to the *Bomoh* before medical advice is sought. The *Bomohs* are generally one of the three types. The first type is the one who supposedly uses Qur'an as a guide for diagnosis and treatment of illness; the second is most closely related to Malay Magic (*Ilmu Batin*), and the third uses herbs and traditional medicines. *Bomohs* are popular in Malaysia among all three races, but the term itself carries a negative connotation because *Bomoh* treatment is not really based on either Qur'anic teachings or scientific methods. When a *Bomoh* fails in his or her appeal or treatment, then another takes over. Malay magic is closely related to Shamanism and educated Malays consider it conflicting with Islamic teachings and avoid such practices. There have been incidences of *Bomoh*-related crimes in the name of religion; however, such persons are treated as criminals under the Malaysian Law. Whereas Eastern States of Peninsular Malaysia are more religiously oriented and their *Bomohs* may be the *Imam* (religious leader) of the community, the other states have *Imams* who are not *Bomohs*.

There are state rehabilitation centers throughout Malaysia that incorporate religious treatments for the drug addicts, prisoners, juvenile delinquents, and so forth in their recovery process. There are also private rehabilitation centers that use solely religious treatment for such populations and are believed to have a better recovery rate compared to state centers, where the religious approach is only secondary to other modern treatment methods. Unlike the West, state centers are run solely by ex-drug addicts. Also, whereas in the West there is a separation of church and state policy especially in government agencies, the public agencies here use religion freely and comfortably. Sound empirical studies on state institution populations are sorely lacking and only a few are published in local or regional psychiatric journals.

Facets of religious psychology are commonly addressed in local magazines as well. Most popular magazines include *Mastika,* which literally means "anthology," and talks about life in the Hereafter, mystic encounters in daily life, and moral values; *Pesona,* meaning "being intrigued," talks about mysticism and human relations; *Majalah Falsafah dan Pemikiran,* which can be translated as "magazine of philosophy and thought," discusses Islamic philosophical concepts addressed by early Muslim scholars like Ghazali, Ibn Rushd, Ibn Sina, and so forth. The *Muslimah* is a women's magazine that has regular columns on Islamic counseling and a question–answer section for personal and social problems. Twenty-four-hour radio programs run by religious institutes offer religious advice, counseling, and discussions on psychological issues. Such programs also invite psychologists to give their views on issues related to human problems.

PSYCHOLOGY OF RELIGION

Psychology has generally received a cold reception in Muslim countries, for several reasons. Foremost among them is its reputation as a secular science, and its appearance of rejection of the spiritual dimension in human beings. In fact, psychology of religion may be even viewed as an atheistic discipline, as many would suspect that this branch of psychology tries to analyze and question people's faith and explain away people's religious beliefs.

A second problem arises because many local people do not even know what psychology is and what the psychology of religion really does. Given these realities, a major problem for the psychology of religion in Malaysia is its recognition as a valid discipline both by the religiously oriented and secular psychologists, academia in general, and society as a whole. Until now, the Malay society has remained strict with religious teachings and is unable to question or analyze religious beliefs. Malays think that religious issues are the responsibility of the state-run religious councils and are a private affair at best, and are therefore reluctant to use psychology for analyzing religious behaviors.

Third, the religious and cultural diversity of the larger Malaysian population poses a conflict of worldviews and a problem of measuring people's religious values. Even within the Malay culture, there is a strong influence of indigenous beliefs and traditions that vary from state to state, and is changing further with modernization taking place here at a very fast rate. For Muslims, quantification of *Iman* (faith) also would be impolite if not outright objectionable. A qualitative analysis on the other hand, may be more acceptable given proper measurement tools that are culturally standardized. This places serious responsibility upon local psychologists who must adapt or develop relevant tests before they venture into the empirical investigations of religious variables on Malay people.

The fourth issue is that of developing an interest in the psychology of religion in academia, where the field could actually take its roots. One way to do this is to train interested psychologists in teaching psychology of religion. Amber Haque is introducing an undergraduate course called *Psychology of Religious Behavior,* starting in July 2002. The reaction of the academic community here remains to be seen, although the initial response was that of curiosity and excitement. A significant portion of the course will address the need for religion in Islamic perspective, varieties of religious behaviors and attitudes in major world religions, and the need for empirical investigations of religious behaviors. This endeavor will hopefully result in research initiatives from students and faculty members. Interesting research areas for psychologists would include nature of religious beliefs, attitudes, and practices of the Malays and the extent to which culture has influenced religion. Why do Malays differ in religious attitudes although they come from the same tradition and hold the same Islamic worldview? What part is religion playing in the immense modernization of Malaysia and the Malay people? What are the differences in religious attitudes among the three important religions in Malaysia given the same national culture and identity? It would also be interesting to do psychological studies on the practice of *Bomohs* and find out why the Malay society has revered them until today and whether the younger generation holds similar attitudes as their ancestors. Organizing conferences at national and international levels and inviting foreign experts for lectures are other ways of creating interest in the local psychologists. However, those teaching the course should familiarize themselves not only in the issues of psychology of religion but also with the sensitivities of the local cultural and religious differences of the Malaysian population. University libraries should buy books and subscribe to international journals related to the discipline. Financial incentives for such research programs at the department and university level may also help.

CONCLUSION

Malaysia is not only culturally but religiously rich and diverse. Islam is the main religion in this country, and certain states comprise a predominantly Muslim population. Although psychology has not really flourished here in the Western sense, almost every aspect of the Malay life is influenced by religion in one way or another, and provides fertile ground for psychological research. The universities are generally open to ideas, and it is up to the existing psychologists to take initiatives in developing their discipline. Collaborative research projects between international and local staff can be highly productive. An indication of increased research is evident from the national conferences, seminars, and published papers in international journals. As religious psychology is quite varied and rich, it appears that the future for the development of the psychology of religion in this country is bright.

REFERENCES

Achoui, M. (1998). Human nature from a comparative psychological perspective. *American Journal of Islamic Social Sciences, 15, 4,* 71–95.

Al-Attas, S. M. N. (1990). *The nature of man and the psychology of the human soul.* Kuala Lumpur: International Institute of Islamic Thought and Civilization.

Al-Attas, S. M. N. (1992). *The concept of religion and the foundation of ethics and morality.* Kuala Lumpur: International Institute of Islamic Thought and Civilization.

Al-Attas, S. M. N. (1993). *The meaning and experience of happiness in Islam.* Kuala Lumpur: International Institute of Islamic Thought and Civilization.

Al-Attas, S. M. N. (1994). *The degrees of existence.* Kuala Lumpur: International Institute of Islamic Thought and Civilization.

Ali, A. H. (1995). Ghazali's contribution to personality theory, *Intellectual Discourse, 3, 1,* 51–64.

Ansari, Z. A. (1992). *Qur'anic Concepts of Human Psyche.* Lahore, Pakistan: International Institute Of Islamic Thought and Institute of Islamic Culture.

Asif, M. M. (2001, July). *Selected works of early Muslim scholars on obsessive-compulsive disorder: A comparative study.* Paper presented at the PSIMA Conference 2001, International Islamic University Malaysia, Kuala Lumpur.

Azhar, M. Z. (2001). Mental Illness and Malay culture: A study of Kelantan Malays. In A. Haque (Ed.), *Mental Health in Malaysia: Issues and Concerns* (pp. 197–219). Kuala Lumpur: University of Malaya Press.

Azhar M. Z. & Varma, S. L. (1995). Religious psychotherapy as management of bereavement. *Acta Psychiatrica Scand, 91,* 233–235.

Azhar, M. Z. & Varma, S. L. (1996). Religious psychotherapy: a proposed model based on The Malaysian experience. *Journal of Federation of Islamic Medical Association, 1,* 64–70.

Azhar M. Z. & Varma, S. L. (1999). Cognitive psychotherapy for inherently religious clients: A two-year follow-up. *Malaysian Journal of Psychiatry, 8,* 19–29.

Badri, M. B. (1979). *The Dilemma of Muslim Psychologists.* London: MWH London Publishers.

Badri, M. B. (2000). *Contemplation: A Psychospiritual Study.* London: Cambridge University Press.

Baki, M. S. (1993). Tingkah Laku Tak Normal [Abnormal Behavior]. In A.H. Othman, *Psikologi Melayu* [Malay psychology] (pp. 344–385). Kuala Lumpur, Malaysia: Dewan Bahasa dan Pustaka.

Faruqi, I. R. (1995). *Islamization of knowledge: General principles and work plan.* Herndon, VA: International Institute of Islamic Thought.

Hatta, S. M. (1995). *Perubatan Psikologi Islam* [Psychological medicine in Islam]. Kuala Lumpur, Malaysia: Dewan Bahasa dan Pustaka.

Hatta, S. M. (2001). Islamic issues in forensic psychiatry and the instinct theory: The Malaysian scenario. In A. Haque (Ed.), *Mental Health in Malaysia: Issues and Concerns* (pp. 181–196). Kuala Lumpur, Malaysia: University of Malaya Press.

Hatta, S. M., Hatta, M. R. & Aliza, I. (1998). Factors influencing the selection of an Islamic healing center. *Malaysian Journal of Psychiatry, 6,* 18–29.

Haque, A. (1977). National Seminar on Islamization of Psychology: Seminar Report. *Intellectual Discourse, 5*(1), 88–92.

Haque, A. (1996). Cognitive restructuring of Muslim psychologists toward developing a firm faith: A prerequisite for Islamization of psychology. *Islamic Thought and Scientific Creativity, 7,* 102–108.

Haque, A. (1998a). International seminar on counseling and psychotherapy: Conference Report, *American Journal of Islamic Social Sciences, 15*(1), 153–157.

Haque, A. (1998b). Psychology and religion: Their relationship and integration from Islamic perspective. *American Journal of Islamic Social Sciences, 15*(4), 97–116.

Haque, A. (1999). Review of Human Nature in Islam by Yasien Mohamad. *Intellectual Discourse, 7*(1), 100–103.

Haque, A. (2000). Psychology and religion: Two approaches to positive mental health. *Intellectual Discourse, 8*(1), 85–98.

Haque, A. (2001a). Interface of psychology and religion: Trends and developments. *Counseling Psychology Quarterly, 14*(4), 1–13.

Haque, A. (2001b). Psychology and religion: Indicators of integration. *North American Journal of Psychology, 3*(1), 61–76.

Haque, A. (2001c). Review of The Psychology of Religion: A Short Introduction by Kate Loewenthal. *American Journal of Islamic Social Sciences, 18*(1), 100–102.

Hoge, D. R. (1996). Religion in America: The demographics of belief and affiliation. In E.P. Shafranske (Ed.), *Religion and the clinical practice of psychology.* Washington, DC: American Psychological Association.

Khan, R. (2001, July). *Effect of prayer as a mode of reducing anxiety in Malay subjects awaiting open heart surgery in Malaysia.* Paper presented at the PSIMA Conference 2001, International Islamic University Malaysia, Kuala Lumpur.

Marzuki, N. A., Ahmad, K., & Ahmad, S (2001, July). *The concept of Mau'izah (advice) in Islamic Counseling: An approach by Al Palimbangi.* Paper presented at the PSIMA Conference 2001, International Islamic University Malaysia, Kuala Lumpur.

Noon, H. M. (2001). Religiosity, values, and social problems in Malaysia. Paper Presented at the PSIMA Conference 2001, International Islamic University Malaysia, Kuala Lumpur.

Othman, A. H. (1993). *Psikologi Melayu* [Malay psychology]. Kuala Lumpur, Malaysia: Dewan Bahasa dan Pustaka.

Philips, B. A. A. (1996). *Ibn Taymeeah's Essay on The Jinn—English translation.* Riyadh, Saudi Arabia: International Islamic Publishing House.

Rahman, F. (1989). *Major themes of the Qur'an.* Kuala Lumpur, Malaysia: Islamic Book Trust.

Salleh, H. (1993). Perubatan Melayu Tradisi. In I. Hussein, A. Deraman, and A.R. Al-Ahmadi (Ed.), *Tamadun Melayu Jilid Dua* [Malay civilization, Vol. II]. Kuala Lumpur, Malaysia: Dewan Bahasa dan Pustaka.

Watanabe, S. (2001, July). Islamic model of mental health and guidance. Paper presented at the PSIMA Conference 2001, International Islamic University Malaysia, Kuala Lumpur.

THE INTERNATIONAL JOURNAL FOR THE PSYCHOLOGY OF RELIGION, *12*(4), 291–292

REVIEW

Terror in the Mind of God: The Global Rise of Religious Violence. By Mark Juergensmeyer. California: University of California Press, 2000. xv + 316 pp. $27.50 cloth, $16.95 paper.

Reviewed by Julius H. Rubin
Saint Joseph College
West Hartford, Connecticut

In this widely cited work, Mark Juergensmeyer explores the emergence of religious terrorism, the acts of violence, occurring throughout the world, that are legitimized by religious worldviews. He reveals a troubling irony: Pious people who are dedicated to a moral vision of reforming the world and who are guided by the ethics of ultimate value, commit atrocities that shake the foundations of post-Enlightenment, secular, civil societies. Sanctioned by divine mandate and imbued with religious conviction and moral absolutism, God's warriors would, in the words of Robert Jay Lifton, "destroy the world to save it."

Marginalized communities throughout the world confront daily violence, poverty, and underdevelopment. In the midst of the accompanying despair, religious terrorist groups establish special communities that strive for collective redemption through a "culture of violence. " They espouse a systematic renunciation of modernity and seek the cataclysmic fulfillment of a religious vision—destroying modernity to restore an idealized image of a past by constructing a social order guided by God's blueprints.

The first half of the book explores these disparate cultures of violence through chapter-length journalistic case studies. Christian examples include American abortion-clinic bombers, Timothy McVeigh and the Christian Identity Movement, and Catholics and Protestants in Belfast. The chapter on Jewish religious violence (in Israel) examines the assassination of Yitzhak Rabin, the attack on the Tomb of the Patriarchs, and Meir Kahane's vision of Zion betrayed. The chapter on Islamic violence explores Hamas and suicide bombings in Israel, as well as Osama Bin Laden's global network that has championed a radical Islamic attack on American targets, including the 1993 bombing of the World Trade Center (and its destruction in 2001 after the book was published). The chapter on Sikh religious violence weaves together the career of Simranjit Singh Mann, the terrorism associated with the Sikh separatist movement, the assassination of Indira Gandhi, and Hindu reprisals. A final chapter introduces a New Age Buddhist new religious movement in Japan—Aum Shinrikyo—and the fusion of weapons of mass destruction with apocalyptic prophecies of the end of the world.

The second half of this work elaborates an explanatory model to ascertain a "logic of religious violence" common to these diverse examples of contemporary religious violence. According to the author, true believers commit horrifying and mind-numbing acts of violence with especial attention paid to the theater of violence—its staging, timing, and performance for live, continuous television coverage. Some targets lack a clear military objective and are chosen as symbolic representations of American political and economic hegemony, like the World Trade Center or the Murrah Federal Building in Oklahoma City.

True believers wage a cosmic war with absolute evil, a war in which their own defeat is unthinkable. Eager to embrace martyrdom and self-sacrifice as soldiers in an epic struggle that they believe will ultimately end in triumph, they demonized and dehumanized the enemy, rendering it into a satanic object that requires annihilation and ritual purification. The chapter "Warrior Power" employs a psychoanalytic perspective, viewing terrorist careers as a means of symbolic empowerment for groups of marginalized young men who face uncertain paths to manhood, sexual identity, and conventional lives.

Juergensmeyer ambitiously surveys the rise of global religious violence in India, Japan, the Middle East, Europe, and America. However, since he is not an expert in any of these culture areas or their religious traditions, he does not offer probing, depth-historical, and multidimensional analyses of these cases. This reader is left unconvinced that generalizations about the logic-of-violence approach can move beyond superficial commonalities. This work does not develop a comparative and historical analysis to identify what is unique to religious, ideological, and cultural groups associated with the rise of religious violence and to those other underprivileged groups that eschew such violence. His analysis of terrorism as an avenue to revitalized masculinity is problematic. Clearly, many in the emerging Al Qaeda network and among the largely Saudi Arabian highjackers in the September 11th attacks do not conform to Juergensmeyer's reductionistic psychoanalytic profile in "Warrior Power."

In the concluding chapter, the author suggests that the desired cure for religious violence involves first separating religion from politics by privatizing and compartmentalizing religion as a voluntaristic institution in a secular society. Second, violence will end when groups heal politics with religion, "when secular authorities embrace moral values, including those associated with religion" (p. 238). It is unclear how the disparate cultures of religious violence, founded upon intolerance of religious differences and committed to the inevitability of cosmic battles and unending fanaticism, will accept a pacified and privatized religious worldview. Equally unclear is how nation-states will determine which moral values to embrace when confronted with competing interest groups who advocate moral absolutism or religious totalitarianism. Sadly, religious violence has incited a possible solution that the author rejects: the militaristic annihilation of terrorists by threatened nation-states. Today, America prosecutes a global war against terrorist groups, terrorist states, and sympathizers, sustained by an ideology that fosters patriotic fervor to destroy all "evil doers" in this "axis of evil."

9 780805 896480